W9-AEZ-000

Mr. Monroe's Message

Also by Frank Donovan

The Medal

The Tall Frigates

The Early Eagles

The Benjamin Franklin Papers

The Unlucky Hero

Juveniles

The Ironclads

The Brave Traitor

The Cutter

327.73
D

Mr. Monroe's Message

THE STORY OF
THE MONROE DOCTRINE

BY

Frank Donovan

ILLUSTRATED

DODD, MEAD & COMPANY

NEW YORK

WINGATE COLLEGE LIBRARY
WINGATE, N. C.

Third Printing

Copyright © 1963 by Frank Donovan
All rights reserved
No part of this book may be reproduced in any form
without permission in writing from the publisher

Library of Congress Catalog Card Number: 63-18822

Printed in the United States of America
by The Cornwall Press, Inc., Cornwall, N. Y.

The quotation from *Abraham Lincoln: The War Years* by Carl Sandburg
is reproduced by courtesy of the publishers, Harcourt, Brace & World, Inc.

The quotation from an article by J. P. McEvoy is reproduced by courtesy of Mrs. J. P. McEvoy.

Contents

29127

Illustrations

Illustrations

following page 110

JAMES MONROE

JOHN QUINCY ADAMS

JAMES POLK

ABRAHAM LINCOLN

GROVER CLEVELAND

THEODORE ROOSEVELT

FRANKLIN ROOSEVELT

JOHN KENNEDY

Mr. Monroe's Message

1

What Is the Monroe Doctrine?

Here is a simple parlor game. Ask the members of any group to list the three most important state documents in American history. The Declaration of Independence will come first. The Constitution will come second. For third place there will be votes for the Monroe Doctrine, the Emancipation Proclamation and, perhaps, the United Nations Charter.

If, at this point, you say, "Aha, I fooled you. The Monroe Doctrine is not a document," you will not be very popular. But you will have made the point that many people who know about the Monroe Doctrine—and probably have some definite opinions on it—do not know what it is.

They need not be embarrassed by this lack of knowledge. They are in good company. During the last one hundred and forty years, oceans of ink have flooded tons of paper in efforts to define the Monroe Doctrine, but there has never been a definition that everybody could agree on. Secretaries of state have made speeches, congressmen have debated, learned international lawyers have rendered opinions, jurists have made decisions, professors have written books, all seeking to define or describe what we call the Monroe Doctrine—but it defies definition. At times, both parties in a debate have called on the Monroe Doctrine to support diametrically opposed contentions.

The Monroe Doctrine is not a law or a legislative act; it is not a treaty, or a charter, or a proclamation, or a manifesto. It is, if you like, an expression of a principle, or a policy on which decisions on some aspects of United States international relationships may be based. But this simple statement is not a complete description. Through the years the situation of the United States in relation to the rest of the world and the rest of the Western Hemisphere has changed, and the principles and policies that guide its conduct have, of necessity, been modified to meet the changing situation. The Monroe Doctrine has changed with the times. It has meant different things to different people at different times in different places. It has not been rigid.

This was not so at the beginning. The basis of what is now called the Monroe Doctrine was contained in a speech made by President James Monroe on December 2, 1823. It was his annual message to the first session of the Eighteenth Congress. In it he reported on the state of the Army, the Navy, and the Post Office. He told the congressmen that, *mirabile dictu*, there would be a surplus in the treasury for 1823, of almost nine million dollars. He condemned the slave trade, recommended that Federal money be spent to repair the Cumberland Road, and commented on a proposed canal to connect Chesapeake Bay and the Ohio River.

There were several paragraphs on foreign affairs. One expressed sympathy for the Greeks who were revolting against the rule of the despotic Turks. One recommended an international agreement to abolish privateering. The remaining two paragraphs on international relations, widely separated in the speech, contained the words that became known as the Monroe Doctrine. The key words in the first paragraph were:

The American continents, by the free and independent condition which they have assumed and maintain, are henceforth not to be considered as subjects for future colonization by any European power.

The key words in the second paragraph were:

In the wars of the European powers in matters relating to themselves we have never taken any part, nor does it comport with our policy to do so. It is only when our rights are invaded or seriously menaced that we resent injuries or make preparation for our defense. With the movements in this hemisphere we are, of necessity, more immediately connected, and by causes which must be obvious to all enlightened and impartial observers. The political system of the allied powers is essentially different in this respect from that of America. . . . We owe it, therefore, to candor, and to the amicable relations existing between the United States and those powers, to declare that we should consider any attempt on their part to extend their system to any portion of this hemisphere as dangerous to our peace and safety. With the existing colonies or dependencies of any European power we have not interfered and shall not interfere. But with the Governments who have declared their independence, and maintained it, and whose independence we have, on great consideration and on just principles, ac-

knowledged, we could not view any interposition for the pur-
pose of oppressing them, or controlling in any other manner
their destiny, by any European power, in any other light than
as a manifestation of an unfriendly disposition towards the
United States.

These statements seem to be quite simple. Mr. Monroe
was expressing his opinion on two specific situations that
existed at the time. He feared that Russia planned to establish colonies on the west coast. He said the United States
would not permit it. He feared that the European powers
were planning to reconquer the Spanish colonies in South
and Central America which had revolted and set up independent governments. He said the United States was opposed to such action.

Mr. Monroe did not know that he was propounding a
doctrine that would become, in the minds of many, the
gospel of American foreign policy. In fact, he would not
have recognized the expression "Monroe Doctrine." In his
lifetime it was never used. For many years, when the speech
was referred to, it was called "Monroe's message" or "Monroe's principles" or "Monroe's pronouncement." The words
"Monroe Doctrine" were first used in a Congressional debate in 1853, thirty years after Monroe had made the
speech. The press picked them up, the public liked their
uplifting, religious connotation, and they have since been
the accepted label for the principles that Monroe set forth
—and for much that was not contemplated in Monroe's ut-
terance. Perhaps the word "doctrine" accounts for some of
the misinterpretation and misunderstanding that developed through the years.

There is a school of thought which holds that Mr. Monroe does not deserve the undying fame which his speech

brought him. Some maintain that he did not write it—that it should be called the Adams Doctrine in honor of John Quincy Adams, Monroe's Secretary of State. These historians claim that Monroe merely held the trumpet while Adams blew the blast. There does not seem to be much merit in this claim. Certainly Adams contributed much to the thinking that was behind the message, as did the other members of Monroe's Cabinet, as well as his friends and mentors Thomas Jefferson and James Madison. But the question of who wrote which word is purely academic, rather like the theological argument of the Middle Ages as to how many angels could stand on the head of a pin.

Actually, the basis of the Monroe Doctrine did not originate with either Mr. Monroe or Mr. Adams. Its genesis goes back beyond the dawn of American independence. Every one of the Founding Fathers who preceded Monroe, with the exception of Benjamin Franklin, had an isolationist point of view. All of them could recall that every war waged in Europe since the New World was settled had been waged also in America, although the causes for the quarrels of the mother countries did not exist in the colonies. English, French, Dutch and Spanish colonists had harried and killed each other in the New World—not because of differences between the settlers, but because of wars between the European countries to which they were subject.

John Adams once said that he "sometimes thought" it would "be the best thing we can do to recall every minister from Europe and send embassies only on special occasions." Thomas Jefferson said, in his inaugural address, "Peace, commerce, and honest friendship with all nations; entangling alliances with none."

George Washington felt so strongly on the matter that he embodied the dogma of isolationism in his Farewell Address in 1796, when he wrote:

Europe has a set of primary interests which to us have none or a very remote relation. Hence she must be engaged in frequent controversies, the causes of which are essentially foreign to our concerns. Hence, therefore, it must be unwise for us to implicate ourselves by artificial ties in the ordinary vicissitudes of her politics or the ordinary combinations and collisions of her friendships and her enmities.

Our detached and distant situation invites and enables us to pursue a different course. If we remain one people under an efficient government, the period is not far off when we may defy material injury from external annoyance; when we may take such an attitude as will cause the neutrality we may at times resolve upon to be scrupulously respected; when belligerent nations, under the impossibility of making acquisitions upon us, will not lightly hazard the giving of provocation; when we may choose peace, or war, as our interest, guided by justice, may counsel.

Why forego the advantages of so peculiar a situation? Why quit our own to stand upon foreign ground? Why, by interweaving our destiny with that of any part of Europe, entangle our peace and prosperity in the toils of European ambition, rivalship, interest, humor, or caprice?

Several years later, Thomas Jefferson, in commenting on future relations with the countries of South America which were then in revolt against Spain, wrote:

But in whatever governments they will end, they will be American governments, no longer to be involved in the never ceasing broils of Europe. The European nations constitute a separate division of the globe; their localities make them a part of a distinct system; they have a set of interests of their own in which it is our business never to engage ourselves.

America has a hemisphere to itself. It must have its separate system of interests; which must not be subordinated to those of Europe. The insulated state in which nature has placed the American continent, should so far avail that no spark of war kindled in the other quarters of the globe should be wafted across the wide oceans which separate us from them and it will be so.

This isolationism was not confined to a few prominent leaders. It was the firm will of the people, repeatedly expressed in Congress. As early as 1783 Congress, in rejecting a proposed League of Neutral Nations, stated that it was "the fundamental policy" of the United States to be "as little as possible entangled in the politics and controversies of European nations." In foreign affairs, from the earliest days, "no entangling alliances" was the watchword. By the man in the street America's foreign policy, for many years, was crudely expressed in the phrase, "We'll leave them alone if they'll leave us alone."

When Monroe made his speech he was standing on the shoulders of all who had gone before and confirming their views in a more definite and forceful manner. Washington had said "the time is not far off when we may defy material injury from external causes." By Monroe's era the time had arrived and he defied the Old World. Jefferson had said, "America has a hemisphere to itself." Monroe added, in effect, "The United States is going to see that it stays that way."

The challenge of the New World to the Old had been inherent since the earliest days of the hardy, self-reliant pioneers who established the first colonies. The challenge was magnified by the development of the different social and economic systems of the New World: the absence of an aristocracy, the lessening of the gulf between the very rich and the very poor, the wider economic opportunity for all and the growth of a large, strong, middle class. The challenge was crystallized by the establishment of a new form of government in the Western Hemisphere—democracy as opposed to monarchy. The Monroe Doctrine was an expression of that challenge of the New World to the Old.

The Monroe Doctrine came to have an almost mystical quality to many as the gospel of all-out isolationism. There were those who felt that every contact with any foreign state should be studied in the light of whether it "violated" the Monroe Doctrine, regardless of whether it had any relation to the points covered in Monroe's speech. In this connection it is interesting to note that the Founding Fathers and their associates were not always consistent in their isolationism. They distrusted Europe, feared her designs, detested her political systems. But they were practical men. In the blackest days of the revolution the Congress was reluctant to seek a mutual defense pact with France. But they sought it and signed it to get the wherewithal to win the war.

Even in this first "entangling alliance" there is evidence of concern about the expansion of foreign holdings in the Western Hemisphere; France was specifically prohibited from taking over "the islands of Bermudas as well as any part of the Continent of North America, which before the Treaty of Paris of 1763, or in virtue of that treaty, were acknowledged to belong to the Crown of Great Britain, or to the United States."

There were other instances of proposed ventures into European alliances on the part of the early isolationists. When France took the Louisiana territory from Spain,

Thomas Jefferson, appalled at the thought of having Napoleon as a neighbor, said we must "marry ourselves to the British nation and fleet." Later Jefferson was concerned lest Cuba fall into the hands of Great Britain. This, he said, "would indeed be a great calamity to us." Within six months before Monroe made his famous speech, Jefferson proposed to him that the United States try to induce Great Britain to sign an agreemnt in which both countries would join "in guaranteeing its [Cuba's] independence against all the world except Spain."

American isolationism was a policy of self-interest. When self-interest dictated a change in policy, the policy could be changed. So it was with the Monroe Doctrine. Although idealists and politicians have talked much of the Doctrine being propounded out of the concern of the United States with freedom and democracy throughout the hemisphere, Monroe said, in his speech, "It is only when our rights are invaded or seriously menaced that we resent injuries or make preparation for our defense." His main concern was what European intervention in Latin America might mean to the peace and security of the United States.

At the time Monroe propounded his doctrine, the self-interest of the United States called for a maintenance of the *status quo*. But at other times and in other situations there was ample precedent for changing that policy. Much of the confusion concerning the Monroe Doctrine has been between those who recognized these facts of international life and those who sought to find, in Monroe's few words, an inflexible guide to all relationships between the United States and the rest of the world.

Another great cause for confusion concerning the Monroe Doctrine is that the United States consistently refused to define it or generally interpret it. All of Europe, for many years, did not recognize or accept the Doctrine. To them, it was no part of international law. It was not a principle that anybody had agreed to as a result of negotiation. It was sometimes a stumbling block in international diplomacy because it might apply in spirit but not in fact. There were many cases in which a European diplomat and an American diplomat held conversations which, shorn of diplomatic language, went something like this.

EUROPEAN DIPLOMAT: I think we can agree on this point.

AMERICAN DIPLOMAT: So do I. Except, of course, we must make the reservation that nothing herein shall be construed as overriding the Monroe Doctrine.

EUROPEAN DIPLOMAT: We might agree to that. What is the Monroe Doctrine?

AMERICAN DIPLOMAT: We won't tell you.

EUROPEAN DIPLOMAT: How can we agree to incorporate the Monroe Doctrine when we don't know what it is? Let us first agree on an interpretation of the Monroe Doctrine and then let us see whether we can work it into the agreement that we are trying to make.

AMERICAN DIPLOMAT: Oh, no. Only the United States can interpret the Monroe Doctrine and we only interpret it as it applies to specific situations as they arise.

That sounds ridiculous. It is, of course, an oversimplification and an exaggeration. But not by much. The unwillingness of the United States to let any international tribunal interpret the Monroe Doctrine or rule on its application had much to do with keeping the country out of the League of Nations and limiting its participation in the Hague Convention.

Through the years the Monroe Doctrine has been blamed for (or credited with, depending on one's point of view) every territorial change in the United States. It has been quoted, either pro or con, as being responsible for the annexation of Texas, the Mexican War, the acquisition of California and New Mexico, the Alaska Purchase, the Spanish-American War, the acquisition of the Philippines and Puerto Rico, the building of the Panama Canal and the annexation of Hawaii.

It has been blamed for many other things. The coolness of the United States toward sending delegates to the Geneva Congress in 1864 to co-operate in the formation of the Red Cross has been attributed to the fact that the work of this international organization of mercy might possibly be an infringement of the Monroe Doctrine. When laws were passed restricting immigration, the United States was referred to as "the great power in North America which closed its doors under the Monroe Doctrine."

At times the Monroe Doctrine has been a political football, at others a political rallying cry. In countless campaign speeches it has been grouped with the Stars and Stripes, motherhood and free enterprise as something that the speaker stood for. Allegiance to the Monroe Doctrine was an assurance that a politician would defend his constituents' rights against the evil intentions and machinations of all foreigners. Being *for* it labeled him as a good, patriotic American, even though neither he nor his hearers knew exactly what being *for* it meant.

During the brief imperialistic period of the United States, around the turn of the twentieth century, the Monroe Doctrine, surprisingly, was quoted to support territorial expansion. During the same period it was twisted to back up "dollar diplomacy." Although there was nothing in Mr. Monroe's speech that would justify the intervention of the United States in the internal affairs of its Latin American neighbors, a corollary was temporarily added to the Monroe Doctrine under which the United States might inject itself into the political affairs of its neighbors to prevent or correct a situation which might bring about foreign interference. And, on occasion, this principle was applied to protect private American investments in Latin America.

As far back as 1914, a famous Secretary of State, Elihu Root, listed some of the past misuses of the Monroe Doctrine in an effort to define it. He said,

A false conception of what the Monroe Doctrine is, of what it demands and what it justifies, of its scope and of its limits, has invaded the public press and affected public opinion within the last few years. Grandiose schemes of national expansion invoke the Monroe Doctrine. Interested motives to compel Central or South American countries to do or refrain from doing something by which individual Americans may profit invoke the Monroe Doctrine. Clamors for national glory from minds too shallow to grasp at the same time a sense of national duty invoke the Monroe Doctrine. The intolerance which demands that control over the conduct and the opinions of other peoples which is the essence of tyranny invoke the Monroe Doctrine. Thoughtless people who see no difference between lawful right and physical power assume that the Monroe Doctrine is a warrant for interference in the affairs of all weaker nations in the New World. Against this suppositious doctrine, many protests both in the United States and in South America have been made, and justly made. To the real Monroe Doctrine these protests have no application.

Mr. Root then went on to define the "real" Monroe Doctrine as he saw it in 1914. What he defined was not exactly what Mr. Monroe saw in 1823, nor what most statesmen of today see in the Monroe Doctrine.

Among South and Central American countries the attitude toward the Monroe Doctrine has varied widely. When Monroe made his speech there was dancing in the streets in Colombia, but only mild interest in Argentina. To the southernmost countries of the Western Hemisphere, England was approximately as close as the United States and a great deal more capable of defending them. In the early years, many Latin American states called upon their neighbor to the north for the protection promised by the Doctrine and, in most cases, the United States responded—and responded effectively. But it must be said that some of the countries to the south were never wildly enthusiastic about a Doctrine that was, presumably, propounded in their interest. Being a practical people they realized that, for much of the nineteenth century, the British fleet was the great deterrent to European aggression in South America. And, since the independence of the South American countries was good business for Britain, the Latin Americans felt that British economic self-interest would be more effective in protecting their rights than United States principles.

As time passed, Latin Americans saw less need for the Doctrine, and resentment against it grew, to become almost universal. There were several reasons for this. Unquestionably, the United States, until quite recently, was supercilious in its relations with its southern neighbors. There was very much the attitude of the big brother who would protect his weaker kin who were not able to take care of themselves—and who would make their decisions for them. As one South American put it: "The Colossus of the North stands ready to hold an umbrella over us. It isn't raining,

WINGATE COLLEGE LIBRARY
WINGATE, N. C.

there is not a sign of a rain cloud on the horizon—and, if it did rain, we are quite capable of holding our own umbrella." And when, at about the turn of the twentieth century, the big brother became a policeman and the umbrella became a big stick, the Latin American resentment was very understandable.

Also, the people of the other Americas were tied more closely to the Old World than to their next-door neighbor by ties of language, religion, social customs and, in the major countries, economics. The *yanquis* did not speak their language, distrusted their religion, did not understand their way of life and did not buy their goods. It was irritating, to say the least, to have a country that was in every respect foreign to them asserting the right to control or dominate certain international relationships of the entire hemisphere.

Another aspect of the inter-hemisphere relations under the Doctrine was that there were different ideas about the meaning of democracy in the North and the South. The United States had its brand, and felt that everybody else should have the same. Many Latin American countries either were not ready for this type of democracy or preferred their own brand. Although the countries to the south are always referred to as the "republics of Latin America" the expression "latinamericandictator" was at one time considered as a single word, like "damyankee" in the Confederacy.

In the United States the Monroe Doctrine has always meant "America for the Americans." But by many cynical Latin Americans it was described as "America for the United States." Monroeism became synonymous with Yankeeism and jingoism and "Yankee fetishism." Typical editorials in the Latin American press have been headlined

"The Yankee Illusion," "The Myth of Monroe," "Monroe-ism, the American Hallucination" and "The United States Against Liberty."

The great protest among the countries of the southern continent toward the Monroe Doctrine was that the United States insisted it was unilateral in principle. Only the United States could apply it. It was only a few years ago that the most recent change took place in the ever-fluid Doctrine, and the United States agreed that it was, to some extent, multilateral. In its most modern form the Monroe Doctrine is not an umbrella held by the United States. It is a principle governing the rights and responsibilities of all the states in the Western Hemisphere, to be mutually applied whenever possible. Despite occasional well-publicized riots, and stones thrown at a United States Vice-President, most of Latin America agrees with this principle, although they still do not like the words "Monroe Doctrine."

At various times during its hectic existence the Monroe Doctrine has been pronounced "dead." Russia's Khrushchev is its most recent self-appointed undertaker, but his condemnation is not new or original. In the past century England's great statesman Disraeli said, "The Monroe Doctrine is one which, with great respect to the government of the United States, is not, in my opinion, suitable to the age in which we live. The increase in the means of communications between Europe and America have made one great family of the countries of the world; and that system of government which, instead of enlarging, would restrict the relations between those two quarters of the globe, is a system which is not adapted to this age." Long after Disraeli's time, England was the first European nation to recognize officially the validity of the Monroe Doctrine.

Generally, the Monroe Doctrine has "died" when there was no immediate need for it and has been reborn when a crisis arose. The best instance of this was in the 1930s. The doctrine was never so dead as it was in the early years of this decade. But in 1940, when Germany's conquest of France raised the specter of Nazi occupation of French territory in the Western Hemisphere, those who had been most loudly declaiming funeral orations a few years before were among the first to cry "violation of the Monroe Doctrine."

There is also a minority opinion among "experts" in the United States that the Monroe Doctrine was not necessary even at the time of Monroe's speech and that it never served any worthwhile purpose. This school of thought flourished during the period of the "debunking" historians that started in the 1920s. They dug into the musty archives of European foreign offices to prove that Monroe's fears were unfounded—that Russia had no intention of enforcing its claims for extended territory on the west coast of North America and that none of the European powers had any thought of trying to regain Spain's South American colonies for the mother country or for themselves. They claim that, had there been no Monroe Doctrine, the states of the Western Hemisphere would have remained free and independent.

This viewpoint would not be worthy of mention except that it has contributed to the confusion concerning the Monroe Doctrine. Whether Monroe's fears were real or fancied at the time, there is no doubt that there have been other times when ambitious European powers would have liked nothing better than to help themselves to poorly defended territory in Latin America—just as they did with most of Africa and much of Asia. This was made clear in the 1860s. As soon as the United States became involved in a civil war which prevented the enforcement of the Monroe Doctrine, France marched into Mexico and established a monarchy and Spain reconquered Santo Domingo. When the Civil War was over and the United States was able to think again of hemisphere defense, they promptly left.

The extent of the gulf between opposing views on the Doctrine is well illustrated by the opening sentences of a current handbook for college debaters, which says:

To the average reader of this book, the Monroe Doctrine is not debatable. And this for one of two reasons:
(1) It exists as a part of our foreign policy. It has existed since 1823. It can now be taken for granted.
(2) Now that Pan-Americanism is in flower, the inter-American unity of spirit destroys all need for the Monroe Doctrine, and as far as the future is concerned, it may be considered a phase of foreign policy of the past.

In short, either the Monroe Doctrine is so alive today that there is no argument about it, or it is so dead that there is no sense talking about it except in terms of history.

The final answer as to whether the Monroe Doctrine is alive or dead must come from the American people, and may be determined from the attitude that they have always had toward it. They may not have understood it, but they firmly believed in it. Whenever it has been applied, rightly or wrongly, the action has had the unqualified support of the majority of the people. One cynical diplomat once said, "All our government has to do to rally the people to the support of any measure . . . is to couple it with the revered title of the Monroe Doctrine."

Call it a myth, or dogma, or fetish or what you will, there is no question that the Monroe Doctrine is an article of belief of the American people—or, at least, the North American people. Mary Baker Eddy, the founder of Christian Science, once said, "I believe strictly in the Monroe Doctrine, in our Constitution, and in the laws of God." Apparently, in Mrs. Eddy's mind, the Monroe Doctrine was some sort of an American Ten Commandments and there were a lot of people who agreed with her.

Obviously, the Monroe Doctrine is not a minor Ten Commandments, nor is it an umbrella or a policeman's club. What, then, is it? Perhaps it may best be understood if it is described simply as a state of mind or a point of view. There have been a lot of changes in the last one hundred and forty years. What we call the Monroe Doctrine has changed with the times. But there has been no change in the state of mind which brought it into being. It grew out of a firm belief in freedom and independence—two things in which Americans still believe.

A British writer once said, "The Monroe Doctrine is like God or religion to a small child—something fearful, something to inspire awe, something, if necessary, to fight for." Is this statement still valid? It certainly is. So long as the people of the Western Hemisphere believe in self-government, the Monroe Doctrine cannot die.

The Russian Menace

History has presented few more impressive spectacles than the gathering which met in Vienna in September, 1814. Four kings were there, and two emperors. They were backed by two hundred and sixteen beribboned and bemedaled diplomats from almost all the powers of Europe, and all were surrounded by the colorful silks and flashing jewels of the ladies of many courts. This was the Congress of Vienna, which had assembled to gloat over the downfall of Napoleon Bonaparte.

There was some difference of opinion as to the objectives of the Congress. The representatives of the smaller nations thought that the primary purpose of the gathering was to settle the many problems that beset Europe as a result of the Corsican's fifteen years of conquest. The Big Four—England, Austria, Russia and Prussia—were more concerned with carving up the melon of Napoleon's empire, which they, with some minor assistance from Spain, Portugal and Sweden, had overthrown. And there was one man who had another idea.

Tsar Alexander of Russia had journeyed from St. Petersburg with supreme confidence that he would dominate the Congress. He had started Napoleon's downfall by burning his own city of Moscow, to leave the French army stranded in the snow. It was his Cossacks who had weakened the Grand Army on their struggle back to civilization, and his Guards had played decisive roles in subsequent battles. It was he, accompanied by the King of Prussia, who had ridden into Paris to witness the French Emperor's abdication. Alexander felt that all of this should give him the right to act as arbiter in the debates of the Congress and to put across a plan which he had thought about, dreamt about and talked about for years—a Plan for Perpetual Peace.

He was so sure of his destiny that he dismissed his minister, Count Tolstoy, and insisted on personally conducting negotiations at the Congress. This was a mistake. The mystical Tsar was no match for such professional diplomats as Austria's Metternich, France's Talleyrand and England's Castlereagh. Also, the Russian's prestige was weakened when the Little Corporal broke out of Elba, surrounded himself with giant grenadiers, and started on a hundred days of renewed conquest. Alexander's troops played no significant part in the allied campaign that ended at Waterloo.

As the Congress of Vienna progressed Alexander's idealistic program was sidetracked. Instead of a Plan for Perpetual Peace he had to be satisfied with a piece of Poland. To restore his prestige and further his plan, Alexander decided on another move, independent of the Congress.

On September 10, 1815 he invited Francis I, Emperor of Austria, and Frederick William III, King of Prussia, to be his guests on the Plain of Vertus, near Châlons. First, there was a review of Russian military might. Long ranks of grenadiers, drilled to robotlike precision, paraded past the assembled monarchs. They were followed by clouds of turbulent, shouting Cossack cavalry. When all were gathered on the field the eyes of the royal watchers turned to the seven altars that had been set up around its edges. In unison the priests at all the altars intoned the imposing ceremony of the Greek Orthodox Mass. The assembled horde thundered the responses.

After this impressive military-religious opening Alexander announced the real business of the meeting. He invited his fellow monarchs to sign what is probably the most unusual document in diplomatic history. It was in the form of a treaty, of which the preamble stated that it was the united policy of the signers:

To manifest before the whole universe their unshakable determination to take as their sole guide, both in the administration of their respective states and in their political relations with other governments, the precepts of religion, namely, the rules of Justice, Christian Charity and Peace.

These principles, far from being applicable only to private life, should on the contrary, govern the decisions of Princes, and direct them in all their negotiations, forming, as they must, the only means of giving permanence to human institutions and remedying their imperfections.

This preamble was followed by three short articles in the same vein, which bound the monarchs to "remain united by the bonds of true and indissoluble fraternity" in conformance with the words of the Holy Scriptures; to "extend a fatherly care and protection" to their subjects; to "consider themselves as members of one and the same Christian nation"; to "confess that the Christian world of which they and their people form a part has in reality no other sovereign than Him to Whom alone rightful power belongs." The document concluded by stating: "All the Powers who shall choose to solemnly avow the sacred principles which have dictated the present act . . . will be received with equal ardor and affection into this Holy Alliance."

Under the eyes of the Russian army, Austria and Prussia signed—though with some confusion and reluctance; confusion because this treaty was not like any other treaty that had ever been drawn—it did not bind anybody to anything that was specific, merely to be good; reluctance because these practical potentates could envision vague but terrifying consequences from an agreement based on nothing but general and widesweeping moral principles.

The agreement came to be known by its final words—the "Holy Alliance." During the next few years every other Christian ruler in Europe signed it except the Prince Regent of Great Britain, and strangely, the Pope. The latter could not sign a religious manifesto of which some of the co-signer were heretics—Protestants. The former excused himself politely on the grounds that the alliance was a personal agreement between rulers, and all acts of the British Crown required the counter-signature of a minister. In justice to Tsar Alexander it must be said that his initial purpose in fathering the Holy Alliance was sincere. He was an idealistic, although impractical, evangelist.

When the United States was invited to join the Holy Alliance, the American ambassador at St. Petersburg was instructed: "Should renewed overtures on this subject be made, Russia would be answered that the organization of our government is such as not to admit our acceding formally to that compact. But it may be added that . . . as a general declaration of principles, the United States not only give their hearty assent to the articles of the Holy Alliance, but they will be the most earnest and conscientious in observing them."

While this was going on in Europe, a great political upheaval was in progress on the other side of the world. The American and French Revolutions had solidified the unrest of the creoles and mestizos, from the Rio Grande to Tierra del Fuego. When Napoleon's invasion of the Spanish peninsula removed the threat of immediate retaliation by Spanish and Portuguese arms, revolt flared in several areas of Latin America. By 1822 almost all of the mainland had freed itself from European rule. Portugal's former colony in Brazil remained intact. Spain's colonial empire was carved into a group of independent states.

Meanwhile, back in Europe, the Holy Alliance was pursuing a purpose which, to freedom-loving Americans, was far from holy. To Alexander and his associates one of the most important "sacred principles" which they had sworn to uphold was the divine right of kings. These absolute monarchs considered this principle so important in the "Christian world" mentioned in their treaty, that Alexander had supported the Turkish Sultan, a Mussulman, in suppressing a revolt of Christian Greeks.

In Spain, liberals had imprisoned King Ferdinand. Even in the eyes of his fellow monarchs, Ferdinand was a despicable ruler. But he was a "legitimate" one, and legitimacy counted above all else. A rearmed France, under the "le-

gitimate" Bourbon Louis XVIII, had been admitted to
the Holy Alliance. French troops marched into Spain and
restored Ferdinand to the throne.

The decision to intervene in Spain had been made at
one of the congresses so dear to the heart of Alexander.
Also on the agenda of this congress, held at Verona, was
the question of Spain's former colonies in America. Should
the powers of the Holy Alliance take action to reconquer
them for the mother country? France's minister, Chateaubriand, had a private plan for extending his country's intervention in Spanish affairs. He proposed a compromise to
Ferdinand under which the Spanish colonies would be reconquered and set up as independent principalities, each
headed by a prince of the House of Bourbon chosen from
the Spanish, French and Italian branches.

Across the Channel, England had become increasingly
disturbed at the course of political affairs in continental
Europe. English diplomacy called for a "balance of power"
on the Continent—not a United States of Europe acting
jointly through a congress. The island kingdom was particularly unhappy about the French intervention in Spain.
It might threaten England's influence in neighboring Portugal. And England was completely opposed to any European action to reconquer any territory in the Western
Hemisphere, either to restore it to Spain or to set it up
under continental princelings.

The primary reason for this was economic. The colonies
in the New World had been pouring the wealth of the
southern part of the Western Hemisphere into the coffers
of Spain and Portugal for three centuries. Until they became independent they could trade only with the mother
countries, sending their goods in Spanish or Portuguese

ships. To maritime England this continent closed to British commerce was irksome. They were quick to seize the commercial advantage when the Latin American colonies revolted. They even helped them to revolt. It is an interesting paradox that, while British armies were saving Spain from Napoleon, British money was aiding the rebels in her colonies. By 1823 Britain was doing a brisk business with the new American states. They did not want to lose it.

There were other, less easily defined, reasons for Britain's support of the Latin American states. One was an interest in the "balance of power" in the New World. And there was a great deal of public sympathy in the insular constitutional monarchy for all people oppressed by autocratic rulers. But the principal reason for Britain's interest in the Western Hemisphere politics could be expressed in pounds, shillings and pence.

On August 16, 1823, the American minister to Great Britain, Richard Rush, was having a rather casual conversation with the British Foreign Secretary, George Canning. During the course of it Rush commented on England's opposition to France's intervention in Spain, and added that should the French armies be successful on the peninsula, there was at least the consolation that "Great Britain would not allow her to go farther and stop the progress of emancipation in the colonies."

Canning's reaction to this rather idle comment surprised Rush. The British minister asked the American ambassador what his government's attitude would be toward going hand in hand with Britain on such a policy. He said that he did not think that any action would be necessary. He thought that France could be held in check by "the simple fact of our two countries being known to hold the same opinion."

This British proposal for an Anglo-American alliance was, at the time, amazing. The city of Washington had scarcely recovered from the torch the British had applied nine years before. The usual British attitude in relations with her former colonies was marked by condescension and arrogance. It was a new experience for the United States to be courted by her mighty ex-mother.

A lesser diplomat than Richard Rush might have been swept off his feet by such flattering attention. Fortunately for America, Rush was a levelheaded Yankee. He stalled for time, saying that he had no instructions on the subject. And he called Canning's attention to the fact that their respective governments had a somewhat different relationship to the Latin American states. The United States had recognized them as sovereign nations. Great Britain had not.

This recognition had taken place in 1822. There had been much agitation for this step throughout the entire revolutionary period in South America. As early as 1810 President James Madison had sent agents to Chile, Venezuela and La Plata (forerunner of Argentina) although their independence was by no means assured. Except for La Plata, they were briefly reconquered after the Duke of Wellington's army drove Napoleon from Spain. In 1817 the Latin liberators again marched, this time successfully.

For the next five years the question of recognition for the states to the south was under almost continual discussion by the Cabinet and Congress. Henry Clay, Speaker of the House of Representatives, was their champion. Surprisingly, John Quincy Adams was the most outspoken opponent. He told Clay that he saw no possibility that the new states would establish free or independent governments. "They are," he said, "not likely to promote the spirit either of freedom or order. . . . They have not the first elements of good or free government."

On another occasion Adams described Latin American politics by saying: "In South America, civil rights, if not entirely out of the question, appear to have been equally disregarded and trampled upon by all parties. Buenos Aires has no constitution and its present rulers are establishing themselves only by the arbitrary banishment of their predecessors. Venezuela . . . has been constantly alternating between an absolute government, a capitulation to Spanish authority, and guerillas black and white, of which every petty chief has acted for purposes of war and rapine as an independent sovereign." Adams correctly prophesied the trend of government of much of Latin America for a century.

But public opinion was behind Clay, and in the beginning, trade or commerce was not a factor. The people of the United States had a fellow feeling for the people in the other Americas in their struggle for liberty and independence. It was a matter of principles and ideals rather than dollars and cents. In fact, the United States stood to lose rather than gain by recognizing the new states. They were doing more business with Spain and Cuba (with or without Spain's permission) than with all of Latin America —a trade which they might lose by antagonizing the mother country.

For several years, although feeling ran high, no action was taken on recognition because the United States was negotiating with Spain for Florida. When these negotiations were successfully concluded, and Florida was ceded in 1821, recognition of the southern states promptly followed.

Throughout the fall of 1823, while Rush's report of his conversation with Canning was slowly sailing across the Atlantic, the British minister continued to press him for a joint statement of policy, even offering to make British recognition of the Latin American states a condition of the deal. Then, in October, the pressure suddenly ceased. When he failed to get prompt action from Rush, Canning had mildly threatened France, and secured a statement from French Foreign Minister Chateaubriand that "France disclaimed, on her part, any intention or desire to avail herself of the present state of the Colonies, or . . . to appropriate to herself any part of the Spanish possessions in America. . . . She abjured, in any case, any design of acting against the Colonies by force of arms." This happened two months before Monroe made his speech. But Monroe did not know it.

When Rush's report reached the desk of his superior, John Quincy Adams, the Secretary of State hastened with it to his superior, James Monroe. Monroe promptly sent it to the man whom he considered *his* superior in matters of state, Thomas Jefferson, requesting him to forward it to one other man on whose opinion Monroe placed great weight, James Madison. It was very natural for the fifth President to lean upon his two predecessors. Monroe was the third, and youngest, of the great triumverate of Virginia Democrats—(who then, confusingly, called themselves Republicans). As a young law student Jefferson had been his advisor and Monroe had worked for the third President as a diplomat; his greatest achievement was the negotiation of the purchase of Louisiana from Napoleon. Later, he had been Madison's Secretary of State.

Unlike Adams, who kept a detailed diary, Monroe did not leave a written record of his thoughts and opinions. His letter to Jefferson is one of the few documents, in his own hand, that throw light on his feelings toward the policy which was to become the Monroe Doctrine. He wrote:

Dear Sir,

I transmit to you two dispatches which were received from Mr. Rush while I was lately in Washington, which involve interests of the highest importance. They contain two letters from Mr. Canning suggesting designs of the Holy Alliance against the independence of South America and proposing a co-operation, between Great Britain and the United States, in support of it, against the members of that alliance. The project aims, in the first instance, at a mere expression of opinion, somewhat in the abstract, but which it is expected by Mr. Canning will have a great political effect by defeating the combination. By Mr. Rush's answers, which are also enclosed, you will see the light in which he views the subject and the extent to which he may have gone.

Many important considerations are involved in this proposition. First, shall we entangle ourselves, at all, in European politics and wars on the side of any power, against others, presuming that a concert, by agreement, of the kind proposed, may lead to that result? Second, if a case can exist in which a sound maxim may and ought to be departed from, is not the present instance precisely that case? Third, has not the epoch arrived when Great Britain must take her stand; either on the side of the monarchs of Europe or of the United States and, in consequence, either in favor of despotism or of liberty; and may it not be presumed that, aware of that necessity, her government has seized on the present occurrence as that which it deems the most suitable to announce and mark the commencement of that career?

My own impression is that we ought to meet the proposal of the British government and to make it known that we would view an interference on the part of the European powers, and especially an attack on the colonies by them as an attack on ourselves, presuming that, if they succeeded with them, they would extend it to us. I am sensible, however, of the extent and difficulty of the question and shall be happy to have yours and Mr. Madison's opinions on it. I do not wish to trouble either of you with small objects, but the present one is vital, involving the high interests for which we have so long and so faithfully and harmoniously contended together. Be so kind as to enclose to him the dispatches, with an intimation of the motive.

With great respect and regard I am, dear sir,

Your friend
James Monroe

Jefferson lost no time in giving the President his definite and forthright views. Monroe's letter was dated October 17, 1823. Jefferson's answer was dated:

Monticello, October 24, 1823

Dear Sir,

The question presented by the letters you have sent me is the most momentous which has ever been offered to my contemplation since that of independence which made us a nation. This sets our compass and points the course which we are to steer through the ocean of time opening on us, and never could we embark on it under circumstances more auspicious.

Our first and fundamental maxim should be never to entangle ourselves in the broils of Europe. Our second, never to suffer Europe to intermeddle in cisatlantic affairs. America, North and South, has a state set of interests distinct from those of Europe, and peculiarly her own. She should therefore have a system of her own, separate and apart from that of Europe. While the last is laboring to become the domicile of despotism, our endeavor should surely be to make our hemisphere that of freedom.

One nation, most of all, could disturb us in this pursuit. She now offers to lead, aid and accompany us in it. By acceding to her proposition we detach her from the band of despots, bring her mighty weight into the scale of free government and emancipate a continent at one stroke which might otherwise linger long in doubt and difficulty. Great Britain is the nation which can do us the most harm of any one, or all, on earth; and with her on our side we need not fear the whole world. With her then we should the most sedulously cherish a cordial friendship; and nothing would tend more to knit our affections than to be fighting once more, side by side, in the same cause. Not that I would purchase even her amity at the price of taking part in her wars. But the war in which the present proposition might engage us, should that be its consequence, is not her war, but ours. Its object is to introduce and establish the American system; of keeping out of our land all foreign powers; of never permitting those of Europe to intermeddle with the affairs of our nations. It is to maintain our own principle, not to depart from it. And if, to facilitate this, we can effect a division in the body of European powers and draw over to our side its most powerful member, surely we should do it.

But I am clearly of Mr. Canning's opinion that it will prevent, instead of provoking, war. With Great Britain withdrawn from their scale and shifted into that of our two continents, all Europe combined would not undertake such a war, for how would they propose to get at either enemy without superior fleets? Nor is the occasion to be slighted which this proposition offers of declaring our protest against the atrocious violations of the rights of nations by the interference of any one in the internal affairs of another so flagitiously begun by Bonaparte, and now continued by the equally lawless alliance, calling itself Holy. . . .

I could honestly, therefore, join in the declaration proposed that we aim not at the acquisition of any of these possessions;

that we will not stand in the way of any amicable arrangement between them and the mother country; but that we will oppose, with all our means, the forcible interposition of any other power as auxiliary, stipendiary, or under any other form or pretext; and most especially their transfer to any power by conquest, cession, or acquisition in any other way.

I should think it, therefore, advisable that the Executive should encourage the British government to a continuance in the dispositions expressed in these letters by an assurance of his concurrence with them as far as his authority goes, and that as it may lead to war, the declaration of which requires an act of Congress, the case shall be laid before them for consideration at their first meeting, and under the reasonable aspect in which it is seen by himself.

I have long been weaned from political subjects and have so long ceased to take an interest in them that I am sensible that I am not qualified to offer opinions on them worthy of any attention. But the question now proposed involves conseqences too lasting, and effects so decisive of our future destinies, as to rekindle all the interest I have heretofore felt on such occassions and induce me to the hazard of opinions which will prove only my wish to contribute still my mite towards anything which may be useful to our country, and praying you to accept it at only what it is worth, I add the assurance of my constant affectionate friendship and respect.

Thomas Jefferson

Jefferson then forwarded the Rush report to Madison with a short letter that has nothing to do with the Monroe Doctrine—but it is an interesting letter.

Th; J. co J. Madison.

I forward you two most important letters sent to me by the President and his letter to me by which you will perceive his prima facie views. This you will be so good as to return to me and forward the others to him.

I have received Trumbull's print of the Declaration of Independence and, turning to his letter, am able to inform you more certainly than I could by memory that the print cost 20D and the frame and glass 12D—say 32D in all.

To answer your question. Pythagoras has the reputation of having first taught the true position of the sun as the center of our system and the revolution of the planets around it. His doctrine, after a long eclipse, was restored by Copernicus and hence it is called either the Pythagorean or the Copernican system. Health and affectionate salutations to Mrs. Madison and yourself.

Monticello, October 24, 1823

The fourth President lost no time in advising his successor. Under date of October 30 he wrote:

Dear Sir,

I have received from Mr. Jefferson your letter to him, with the correspondence between Mr. Canning and Mr. Rush, sent for his and my perusal and our opinions of the subject of it.

From the disclosures of Mr. Canning it appears, as was otherwise to be inferred, that the success of France against Spain would be followed by attempts of the Holy Alliance to reduce the revolutionized colonies of the latter to their former dependence.

The professions we have made to these neighbors; our sympathy with their liberty and independence; the deep interests we have in the most friendly relations with them; and the consequences threatened by a command of their resources by the great powers confederated against rights and reforms of which we have given so conspicuous and persuasive example; all unite in calling for our efforts to defeat the meditated crusade. It is particularly fortunate that the policy of Great Brittain, although guided by calculations different from ours, has presented a co-operation for an object the same with ours. With that co-operation we have nothing to fear from the rest of Europe; and with it the best reliance on success to our just and laudable views. There ought not be any backwardness therefore, I think, in meeting her in the way she has proposed; keeping in view, of course, the spirit and forms of the Constitution in every step, if those short of war should be without avail.

It cannot be doubted that Mr. Canning's proposal, although made with the air of *consultation* as well as concert, was founded on a predetermination to take the course marked out whatever might be the reception given here to his invitation. But this consideration ought not to divert us from what is just and proper in itself. Our co-operation is due to ourselves and to the world: and whilst it must ensure success in the event of an appeal to force, it doubles the chance of success without that appeal.

It is not impossible that Great Britain would like best to have the sole merit of being the champion of her new friends notwithstanding the greater difficulty to be encountered, but for the dilemma in which she would be placed. She must in that case leave us either as neutrals to extend our commerce and navigation at the expense of hers, or make us enemies by renewing her paper blockades and other arbitrary proceedings on the ocean. It may be hoped that such a dilemma will not be without a tendency to check her proneness to unnecessary wars.

Why the Brtish Cabinet should have scrupled to arrest the calamity it now apprehends by applying to the threats of France and Spain the "small efforts" which it scruples not to employ on behalf of Spanish America, is best known to itself. It is difficult to find any other explanation than that *interest* in the one case has more weight in her casuistry than principle had in the other.

Will it not be honorable to our country, and possibly not altogether in vain, to invite the British government to extend the avowed disapprobation of the project against the Spanish colonies to the enterprise of France against Spain herself; and even to join in some declaratory act in behalf of the Greeks? On the supposition that no form could be given to the act clearing it of a pledge to follow it up by war, we ought to com-

pare the good to be done with the little injury to be appre-
hended to the United States shielded as their interests would
be by the power and the fleets of Great Britain united with
their own. These are questions, however, which may require
more information than I possess, and more reflection than I
can now give them.

What is the extent of Mr. Canning's disclaimer to "the remaining possessions of Spain in America?" Does it exclude
future views of acquiring Porto Rico, etc., as well as Cuba? It
leaves Great Britain free, as I understand it, in relation to
Spanish possessions in other quarters of the globe.

I return the correspondence of Mr. R. and Mr. C. with as-
surances of the highest respect and sincere regard.

James Madison

With this correspondence from two ex-Presidents at hand
six weeks before he made his speech, Monroe took the matter up with his Cabinet, which contained a future President
in John Quincy Adams. No other government policy has
ever had, in its formulation, the attention of so many chief
executives. This was the background against which one
aspect of the Monroe Doctrine was developed—nonintervention in Latin America. In connection with the other
aspect—no colonization—Tsar Alexander was also the potential villain.

In 1741 Vitus Bering, a Dane in the Russian service, discovered America from the east when he landed on the coast
of Alaska. Bering died on the voyage home, but his crew
returned to Russia with tales of swarms of fur-bearing
animals on the northern coast and samples of a new fur
—sea otter. When the Russians introduced the skin of this
soft, gentle creature to the Chinese it promptly became an
oriental status symbol. To be a mandarin of distinction one
required a cap, collar or mittens of sea otter, regardless of

cost. The northern coast of the Western Hemisphere was a treasure-trove of fur.

As word of the find in furs spread, Spain's long supremacy in the Pacific was challenged by fur-hunting vessels from England, France, Holland, the North American Colonies and Russia. By 1799 the latter had established bases at Kodiak and Sitka for the Russian-American Company, a privately owned, official monopoly to which Alexander granted all trading rights north of latitude 55 and permission to establish settlements on either side of that line in territory not occupied by other powers. In 1812 they established such a settlement, Rossiya—usually called Fort Ross —eighty miles north of present-day San Francisco.

The Russians were plagued by poachers, mostly Yankee, in what they considered their proper sphere of northern waters. In 1821 Alexander issued a ukase to correct this, which moved the Russian line south to 51 degrees north latitude—a point slightly north of the present United States-Canadian boundary.

Alexander's decree put three countries in competition for the same territory. When Spain ceded Florida she had also renounced rights on the Pacific Coast north of 42 degrees. By an agreement made with Great Britain in 1818 the United States and England jointly administrated the territory from 42 degrees to an indeterminate northern boundary. Now Russia proposed to move into a large part of this area.

Meanwhile, John Quincy Adams had become convinced that there should be *no* foreign colonies in North America. In a cabinet meeting in 1819 he said that the world must be "familiarized with the idea of considering our proper dominion to be the continent of North America. From the time when we became an independen people it was as much a law of nature that this should become our pretension as that the Mississippi should flow to the sea. Europe shall find it a settled geographical element that the United States and North America are identical."

The section of the Monroe Doctrine dealing with no further colonization unquestionably stemmed from Adams. The Tsar's decree was the subject of diplomatic discussion in St. Petersburg by both the American and British ambassadors. For the guidance of the American ambassador, Monroe's Cabinet agreed that he should be advised that the United States would recognize Russia's claims north of 55 degrees. In forwarding these instruction to Middleton, American ambassador at St. Petersburg, Adams made the United States position a little stronger by saying: "There can be, perhaps, no better time for saying, frankly and explicitly, to the Russian government that the future peace of the world, and the interest of Russia herself, cannot be promoted by Russian settlements on any part of the American continent."

Then, in conversation with Russia's ambassador to Washington, he went much further and said that "we should contest the right of Russia to any territorial establishment on this continent and that we should assume distinctly the principle that the American continents are no longer subjects for any new European colonial establishments." This conversation took place on July 17, 1823. Six months later, when Adams prepared the notes on the foreign policy section of Monroe's speech, he picked up almost the exact words he had spoken to the Russian ambassador, and Monroe used them without change.

Monroe felt that the threat of the Holy Alliance and the

situation of the Latin American states was a subject of great importance, but he does not seem to have been much concerned about the no-colonization policy. At least, there is no record that he ever discussed it with anybody. Adams' very detailed diary does not mention such a discussion, and J. C. Calhoun, Monroe's Secretary of War, stated positively that it never came up at a Cabinet meeting. Apparently, when Adams proposed it, Monroe went along with his Secretary of State without realizing that he was propounding an idea that would make history in the future foreign policy of the United States.

The South American question was the subject of long and heated debate in the Cabinet. Supported by the advice of Jefferson and Madison, and the opinion of at least three Cabinet members, Monroe may have, at first, favored going along with the joint declaration with England, proposed by Canning. Adams opposed this. He was sure that the new southern states were in no danger from the Holy Alliance, and he distrusted Canning's offer. He made the point that, since England had not recognized the newly independent states, there was nothing to prevent her from changing her mind about the alliance with America if self-interest so dictated.

There was nothing about South America in the notes that Adams gave the President for the foreign policy section of his speech. However, he was quite willing to make the situation the subject of a state paper of some kind. In a Cabinet meeting on November 7 he said that the subject presented "a very suitable and convenient opportunity for us to take our stand against the Holy Alliance, and at the same time to decline the overture from Great Britain. It will be more candid as well as more dignified to avow our principles explicitly to Russia and France, than to come in as a cock-boat in the wake of the British man-of-war."

An exact determination of "who did what" in relation to Monroe's message can be carried no further. Unlike Adams, Monroe left no detailed records. Adams tells the part that he played in his diary—a journal in which he never minimized his own accomplishments. It seems that the no-colonization idea was strictly an Adams cause which had Monroe's approval. The Latin American aspect was Monroe's principal concern. He bravely faced what he considered a real and imminent threat to Western Hemisphere peace and security with a ringing pronouncement which put the American David squarely in the path of the European Goliath.

Considering all that has happened since, the immediate world reaction to Monroe's message was surprisingly mild. The venerable Lafayette, an honorary citizen of the United States, was almost alone in endorsing it with the statement that it was "the best little bit of paper that God had ever permitted any man to give to the world." Most of Europe's diplomats condemned it with such words as "blustering," "monstrous," "arrogant" and "haughty."

But there was no formal protest from any European nation. France's Chateaubriand said that the no-colonization clause "ought to be resisted by all the powers possessing either territory or commercial interest in that hemisphere." No such action was taken. Austria's Metternich penned a blast which charged the United States with "a new act of revolt, more unprovoked, fully as audacious, and no less dangerous than the former." But he proposed no action. Russia's ambassador at Washington wanted to denounce the speech in ringing terms but Alexander told him: "The document in question enunciated views and pretentions so exaggerated . . . that it merits only the most profound contempt." From Berlin and Madrid came only silence.

The Tsar's word "contempt" is the key to the slight European interest in the firm position that the United States had taken. No one in Europe believed that the United States would go to war on a matter of principle. In Europe's eyes, Americans were purely materialistic. And if the little nation was willing to fight, no foreign power feared it. Despite the dramatic victories of its few frigates in the War of 1812, the tiny American navy had been easily swept from the seas when Britain assembled her power.

Perhaps the only immediate effect of the message on European policy at the time was that it gave Canning an excuse to refuse to participate with the Holy Alliance in a new congress on the subject of the South American colonies. "The Congress," he said, "was broken in all its limbs before, but the President's speech gives it the *coup de grâce*."

Canning reacted with annoyance and jealousy. His thunder had been stolen. He feared that the United States, rather than Great Britain, would get all the credit in Latin America. He hastened to publish the agreement which he had secured from the French in all the South American capitals in an effort to maintain British prestige. Later, he sought to claim credit, at least at home, with a dramatic statement to the House of Commons, saying, "I called the New World into existence to redress the balance of the Old."

The important reaction to Monroe's message was that of the people of the United States. His challenge to the Old World, his reiteration of the theme, "America for the Americans," hit a responsive note on the great organ of public opinion. Again, the effect was best described by an English diplomat in Washington:

The message seems to have been received with acclamation throughout the United States. . . . The explicit and manly tone . . . has evidently found in every bosom a chord which vibrates in strict unison with the sentiments so conveyed. They have been echoed from one end of the union to the other. It would indeed be difficult, in a country composed of elements so various, and liable on all subjects to opinions so conflicting, to find more perfect unanimity than has been displayed on every side in this particular point.

3

The First Demise

When the Lion of England replaced the Lilies of France in Canada at the end of the Seven Year's War, a young French officer named Louis Antoine de Bougainville sought to offset his country's loss by establishing a colony elsewhere in the New World. At his own expense he outfitted a frigate and a sloop and set sail from St. Malo. His voyage ended on a bleak, barren, treeless island in the Atlantic, three hundred miles northeast of the Straits of Magellan. He called this, and the neighboring islands, the Malvinas. In 1764 he established a colony there. He left twenty-eight people, nine cattle, ten pigs, three horses and a goat and went back to France to tell his countrymen of their new possession.

Bougainville either did not know about or did not care about a treaty between France and Spain which gave the latter a monopoly in South Atlantic waters. Reluctantly, the French King told him to turn his colony over to the Spaniards. He journeyed to Madrid, sold his South Atlantic venture for 25,000 pounds.

Meanwhile, a British captain named John Byron—better known by the engaging nickname of "Foulweather Jack" —had landed on the other side of the Malvinas, erected a flagtaff, raised the Union Jack and claimed possession of what he called the Falkland Islands for the Crown of Great Britain.

By 1769 the English had added a blockhouse to their flagpole and stationed a ship there. When a Spanish schooner came around to their side to make a survey, the English sent her home with a letter telling the Spaniards to get out. Two days later she returned with a letter from the Spanish governor telling the English to get out. This exchange of eviction notices was twice repeated before five Spanish frigates sailed into the English bay and compelled the British to leave.

Back in Europe this highhanded action brought England and Spain to the brink of war until a compromise was reached under which Spain agreed to restore the block-house to the British without affecting "in any way the question of her anterior right of sovereignty over the Malvinas." The English went back to the Falklands and raised their flag. Three years later they departed again, leaving a lead seal on the blockhouse saying: "Be it known to all nations that Falkland's Islands, with this fort, the storehouse, wharfs, harbours, bays and creeks thereunto belonging, are the sole property of His Most Sacred Majesty, George the Third, King of Great Britain, France and Ireland, Defender of the Faith."

The Spanish remained in undisputed possession of the

islands until 1816, when ownership passed to Argentina after that country won its independence. Argentina gave a man named Louis Vernet permission to expand the settlement on the Falklands. By 1831 he was doing a flourishing business provisioning ships en route to the Pacific and exporting salt beef and fish. At this time the South Atlantic sealing trade was booming. Vernet claimed a monopoly of this and ordered all other vessels off. When the American sealer *Harriet* ignored his order, he captured it and took the vessel to Buenos Aires where her captain, John Davison, was to be tried. Davison escaped, made his way to Montevideo, went aboard the United States corvette *Lexington* in that harbor, and told his story to the vessel's commander, Lieutenant Silas Duncan.

The *Lexington* promptly sailed for the Falklands. Duncan sacked Vernet's settlement, spiked the guns, fired the magazine, roughed up the inhabitants and departed with seven of the principal settlers in irons to take them back to the United States to be tried for piracy. Shortly after the *Lexington* left, the British sloop *Clio* sailed into the harbor, and her captain calmly announced that he was taking possession of the islands for Great Britain.

In the broad pageant of American history the early tribulations of two tiny islands near the Antarctic are of no importance—except that they represent the only colony that has been established by a European power in the Western Hemisphere since Monroe made his famous speech. And the United States did nothing about it.

Detractors of the Monroe Doctrine make much of this little incident to show that the United States made no effort to enforce the principle of no colonization ten years after it had been stated, nor to help a Latin American state against

foreign aggression. Defenders of the Doctrine allege that, at
the time, there was some confusion as to Argentina's rights
in the matter. Cynics point out that Argentina had made
a claim against the United States for the depredations of
Lieutenant Duncan which the northern republic would
have to pay if it recognized the sovereignty of its southern
neighbor in the islands. The United States never did pay
the claim.

The fact of the matter seems to be that the ownership
of these tiny dots of distant land could not possibly represent a threat to the United States. In Monroe's words, "our
rights" were not "invaded or seriously menaced." It was
then considered that the protection of "our rights" was the
sole purpose of Monroe's pronouncement. And it was not
recognized as a "doctrine." It was a principle to be applied
when the situation seemed to warrant its application.

Also, there was some feeling that Monroe's message applied only to the particular dangers toward which it was
addressed—the intervention of the Holy Alliance in Latin
America, and Russian colonization on the Pacific coast. The
former never materialized. The latter was amicably settled
by the negotiations which had been in progress before
Monroe made his speech, and without reference to the
Monroe Doctrine. Apparently, Tsar Alexander had issued
his ukase rather idly, under pressure from commercial interests, and had no intention of making an issue of it.
Russia readily agreed to setting the southern boundary of
their sphere at latitude 54 degrees, 40 minutes north, the
present boundary of Alaska.

The Russian colony at Fort Ross remained for eighteen
years after the Monroe Doctrine—a pleasant, peaceful little
place. Architecturally, it was far more impressive than the

nearby Spanish presidios. Inside the stockade were a chapel, barracks, officers quarters, a storehouse, a jail and a fine house for the commandant with the rare luxury of window glass. Outside the walls were the neat houses of the Russian settlers, the flat cabins of the Aleut hunters brought from Alaska and the cone-shaped huts of the California Indians. The whole was surrounded by well-tilled fields, orchards and vineyards.

The end was rather sad. The near extinction of the sea otter made the colony unprofitable. The Russians tried to make a living by logging the giant redwoods of the nearby forest, but the market was slim. Still, the Russians lived graciously. The officer's ladies dressed elegantly for dinners in an open pavilion in the orchard, hung with the imperial colors. The wife of the last commandant, a beautiful, blonde young Princess, tended her plants in the only glass conservatory in the west. A visiting Frenchman wrote that it was the most civilized place he had visited, with "a choice library, French wines, a piano and a score of Mozart."

During the late 1830s American squatters started to move in around Fort Ross on land that the Russians had purchased from the Indians. The Russians had no choice but to leave or to fight them. They left in 1842, after selling their buildings, stock and equipment to John Sutter of gold rush fame. Princess Helena, wife of the commandant, implored Sutter not to destroy her conservatory, but although some of the buildings were reassembled at Sutter's Mill, the American carpenters were unable to put the conservatory back together. And so ended the Russian menace. Nobody ever suggested applying the Monroe Doctrine to the little Russian colony above the Golden Gate.

Within sixty days after Monroe made his speech, Henry

Clay proposed to interpret the principle of nonintervention into law by introducing into the House of Representatives a resolution supporting it. The resolution never came to a vote, and Clay later withdrew it, saying that circumstances had changed so that it was no longer necessary. Even the foremost champion of Latin America felt that the message applied to a specific situation—it was not a lasting doctrine.

Seven months after Monroe's speech, Colombia, fearful of French intervention, quoted the Doctrine in asking whether the United States would "enter into a treaty of alliance with her to save America from the calamities of a despotic system." Secretary of State Adams brushed off the request by saying that such a decision would be up to Congress. He continued, with a masterpiece of diplomatic weaseling, to say that "the United States could not undertake resistance by force of arms, without a previous understanding with those European powers whose interest and whose principles would secure from them an active and efficient co-operation in the cause." In short, the United States would not act except in conjunction with England. This from the man who had said, a few months before, that the United States should not be "a cock-boat in the wake of a British man-of-war."

Brazil fared no better than Colombia in seeking a defensive alliance based on Monroe's principles. Brazil asked whether, in the event that some European power was to assist Portugal in attempting to reconquer her, "the United States would be bound to put into practice the policy laid down in the said message," and suggested a treaty to this effect. Clay, now Secretary of State under President John Quincy Adams, replied that "such a treaty would be inconsistent with the policy which the United States have heretofore prescribed to themselves."

The best description of the Monroe Doctrine, as it was understood three years after the event, involved Mexico. Joel Poinsett, newly appointed minister to the southern republic, was carried away with enthusiasm in his efforts to create good will in Mexico City. He told the Mexican Secretary of State that the United States had "openly declared their determination not to permit any other nation to interpose with armed hand between Spain and the Americas."

When news of this reached Washington, Congress demanded a statement from President Adams as to "whether the United States had, in any manner, made any pledge to the governments of Mexico and South America." Through Secretary Clay, Adams replied with a definite statement of his administration's interpretation of the Monroe Doctrine.

The United States have contracted no engagements, nor made any pledge to the governments of Mexico and South America, or to either of them, that the United States would not permit the interference of any foreign power with the independence or form of government of those nations, nor have any instructions been issued authorizing any such engagement or pledge.

All apprehensions to which Mr. Monroe alludes, of an interference by the allied powers of Europe to introduce their political systems into this hemisphere, have ceased. If, indeed, an attempt by force had been made by allied Europe to subvert the liberties of the southern nations on this continent, and to erect upon the ruins of their free institutions monarchial systems, the people of the United States would have stood pledged, in the opinion of their Executive, not to any foreign state, but to themselves and to their posterity, by their dearest interests and highest duties, to resist to the utmost such attempt; and it is to a pledge of that character that Mr. Poinsett alone refers.

Thus, three years after it was propounded, the Monroe Doctrine died for the first time. It would remain dead for the next two decades. Until the mid 1840s virtually nothing was heard of Monroe's magic words in the press, or in Congress. Latin America, too, considered it a dead issue. If they were to have outside help against the powers of Europe, they looked to Great Britain, the mistress of the seas, not the weak republic to the north.

Through the 1830s there were several "violations" of the Monroe Doctrine, other than in the Falkland Islands, mostly by Great Britain. At that time most of the isthmus was embraced in the recently formed Republic of Central America. At Belize, in what is now Honduras, the English had a small settlement, in which their nationals had certain rights under a treaty with Spain which antedated the Monroe Doctrine. After 1823 they started to expand their territory and, in 1833, replied to a protest of the Republic of Central America by declaring that they had exclusive jurisdiction over the extended area, which became British Honduras. The foreign minister of Central America appealed to the United States saying, "Suffer me to remind you that it has always been the policy of the United States that there should be no European settlements upon the American continent." He was told by John Forsyth, Andrew Jackson's Secretary of State, that "it was not deemed expedient to interfere in the matter."

The English later seized a large island off the coast of Honduras which was clearly part of the Republic of Central America, again without protest from the United States. They also annexed a strip of future Nicaragua by declaring that the Mosquito Indians who inhabited it were under British protection. They set up the Kingdom of Mosquitia, crowned a painted savage who swore allegiance to the British Crown, and seized the mouth of the San Juan River for their native stooge. Again there was no protest from the United States. The English behaved as though the Monroe Doctrine did not exist. So did the United States.

During all these years the United States had little interest in, and little contact with, Latin America. Americans were pushing westward on their own continent. That was where the future lay. It was this westward expansion that revived the Monroe Doctrine in the 1840s.

The growing number of Americans in Texas had led to the separation of that province from Mexico in 1836—an independence which Americans had bloodily maintained at the Alamo and the Battle of San Jacinto. Texas promptly applied for admission to the Union, which led to eight years of wrangling in the United States Senate, where the representatives of the northern states vigorously opposed the acquisition of this large slave-holding territory. During this time, France and England were making strenuous efforts to prevent the annexation of Texas by the United States. They even discussed guaranteeing her independence, singly or jointly, so as to, in effect, make Texas a European protectorate. Their concern was with the principle, so dear to the hearts of European diplomats, of the "balance of power" in the Western Hemisphere. During the heated Congressional debates on Texas annexation the words of Monroe were remembered and repeateadly quoted.

And, in addition to Texas, there was Oregon. The northwest territory was still administered under the joint Anglo-American agreement of 1818, but American settlers were thronging into Oregon. There was a demand for a settlement of the boundary line. The incumbent President, James Polk, had run on a campaign slogan of "fifty-four forty or fight." As popular sentiment ran high the message of Monroe was quoted by public and press to denounce any extension of Britain's colony on the north.

And there was California. In this northern province Mexico exerted little influence in the early 1840s. The Californians were an independent lot, not readily subject to distant authority. It was obvious that California would not long remain a part of the republic to the south. Its future was of vital concern to the United States. She wanted it—had offered to buy it, but Mexico had turned the bid down. Also, there was suspicion and fear that England had her eye on it. The American consul in Monterey reported the presence of sinister British agents, who, he was sure, were plotting with Californians to declare for independence and then place themselves under the protection of Great Britain.

All of this led President Polk to tell influential Senator Benton of Missouri that he planned to reassert "Mr. Monroe's Doctrine against permitting foreign colonization, and that in doing this he had California and the fine bay of San Francisco as much in view as Oregon." Polk did restate Monroe's message in his own first annual address to Congress on December 2, 1845, the twenty-second anniversary of the original speech. After repeating Monroe's words relative to non-colonization, he continued:

> This principle shall apply with greatly increased force should any European power attempt to establish any colony in North America. In the existing circumstances of the world the present is deemed a proper occasion to reiterate and reaffirm the principle avowed by Mr. Monroe and to state my cordial concurrence in its wisdom and sound policy. The reassertion of this principle, especially in reference to North America, is at this day but the promulgation of a policy which no European power should cherish the disposition to resist. Existing rights of every European nation should be respected but it is due alike to our safety and our interests that the efficient protection of our laws should be extended over our whole territorial limits, and that it should be distinctly announced to the world as our settled policy that no future European colony or dominion shall with our consent be planted or established on any part of the North American continent.

Polk's speech not only brought the Doctrine back to life, but was the first "revision" of it. His wording would later lead to endless debate as to how extensively the Doctrine had been changed by his interpretation. In his speech he referred only to North America; he did not mention the Western Hemisphere. Was it to be inferred from this that the United States no longer supported the principle of nonintervention in the other Americas? Some said yes. Others pointed out that the particular concerns which led him to reiterate the document at that time related to North America, and that in using the words "especially in reference to North America" he had not changed the basic policy toward affairs in the other Americas. Such legalistic quibbling is of no interest except to indicate the confusion that was already starting to develop as to the meaning of the Monroe Doctrine.

Polk made another contribution to the interpretation of the Doctrine. Monroe had thought of European intervention solely in terms of armed force. Polk extended it to mean diplomatic intervention. He wrote:

Jealousy among the different sovereigns of Europe . . . has caused them anxiously to desire the establishment of what they term the "balance of power." It cannot be permitted to have any application on the North American continent, and especially to the United States. We must ever maintain that people of this continent alone have a right to decide their own destiny. . . . We must never consent that European powers shall interfere . . . because it might disturb the "balance of power" which they may desire to maintain upon this continent.

Polk had in mind the possible guarantee of Texas independence by France or England. His position was promptly rejected in Europe. Said the French Prime Minister: "The maxim is a strange one. The United States is not the only nation of North America. There are, on the North American continent, other independent nations. . . . These states have the same right to seek or reject alliances, to form such political combinations, as appear to them to accord with their interests. The proximity . . . of the United States cannot in any degree limit their independence or their rights."

Polk soon made it clear that the Monroe Doctrine still applied to Latin America, at least in principle. He also made it clear that the principle would be applied only when, as and if the United States wanted to, or was able to, apply it.

In Argentina an odious dictator named Juan Manuel de Rosas had been muddying up the waters of his neighbors for some time. He wanted to put his own man in as President of Uruguay. By 1845 this had developed into a vicious war which threatened Uruguayan independence. Neighboring Brazil was very much concerned. She sent an emissary, not to the United States, but to England and France to request help in thwarting Rosas' designs. After unsuccessfully attempting peaceful mediation, the two European nations sent a fleet to blockade the Argentina coasts, seized Argentinian naval vessels and the island of Martin Garcia, sent a punitive expedition up the Paraná River, and sought to induce Paraguay to forcibly oppose Rosas.

Although there was no thought that the purpose of the French and English was either conquest or colonization, their intervention was a clear violation of the Monroe Doctrine. No one knew where it might end, but a European protectorate over Uruguay was not unlikely, and it was certainly an interference in the political affairs of South America.

In this whole situation the United States was ignored, until the American consul at Buenos Aires vigorously protested against the Anglo-French blockade. When England complained about his aggressive attitude he was recalled and a more moderate man was sent to replace him. In his instruction to the new minister, Secretary of State Buchanan gave a good example of the attitude toward the practical application of the Monroe Doctrine at that time. He said, "The late annual message of the President to Congress has so clearly presented the great American doctrine in opposition to the interference of European governments in the internal concerns of the nations of this continent that it is deemed unnecessary to add another word upon the subject. That Great Britain and France have flagrantly violated this principle by their intervention in La Plata is manifest to the whole world." After this forceful preamble, Buchanan ruefully concluded by saying that "existing circumstances render it impossible for the United States to take part in the present war."

Buchanan's last words cover many situations to which detractors of the Doctrine have pointed with scorn because it was not applied when it was clearly applicable. But the Doctrine was never the sole instrument of foreign policy of the United States. There were other practical matters to be considered. In this instance, Anglo-American relations were already somewhat strained by the Oregon negotiations. To endanger this operation in the interests of activity on behalf of far-off Uruguay would have been the height of folly. Also, war with Mexico was brewing. It was no time for the United States to become involved in a military operation at the other end of the hemisphere.

This situation raised another point that would become increasingly clear in the development of the Doctrine. Although, as a principle, it might have equal force throughout the Western Hemisphere, in practice its force was more equal in some places than in others. At that time it applied more forcefully to neighboring Oregon, California and Texas than it did to distant Argentina and Uruguay.

For fifteen years following Polk's reassertion of the Doctrine it was seldom out of the limelight. References to it in Congressional debate and in diplomatic correspondence were frequent. It was during this era that it became known as the "Monroe Doctrine" and, almost coincidental with its new title, the public attitude toward it as a somewhat mystical, patriotic dogma started to take shape.

For a time after Polk's message some Latin American

countries again sought support from the United States through an appeal to the Doctrine. The first instance of this was in 1846. An ousted Ecuadorian President, Juan José Flores, had fled to Madrid to seek the support of Maria Christina for the re-establishment of a monarchy in Ecuador with her son, Don Juan, as king and Flores as his minister. Christina loaned him some money. He privately enlisted some Spanish troops and went to England to buy ships to transport his expeditionary force.

The comic-opera aspect of Flores' adventure was generally apparent, but not to Eucador or neighboring Peru. Ecuador appealed to the United States, mentioning "the solemn protests that have at all times, and particularly at present, been made by the cabinet of Washington against all European intervention in the political affairs of America." Peru, seeking to get ships from the United States to support her neighbor, reminded the United States that they "have proclaimed long since to Europe that all attempts to interfere in domestic affairs . . . would be viewed as an act of hostility against the American people." The threatened Flores invasion had petered out before their appeals were made, and no action on the part of the United States was necessary. But their requests were an indication that America's reassertion of the Doctrine did not fall on deaf ears in Latin America.

The English continued to ignore the Doctrine in Central America. They extended their rule from one island off the coast of Honduras to several—calling them the Bay Island colony. They again expanded the territory of their tame Mosquitoes, extending it down into New Granada—present-day Colombia—and seizing Greytown at the mouth of the San Juan River. This brought a protest to Washington from Nicaragua, quoting the Monroe Doctrine. To this appeal Secretary Buchanan rather plaintively replied, "What can the United States do to resist such European interference whilst the Spanish American republics continue to weaken themselves by division and civil war and deprive themselves of the ability of doing anything for their own protection?"

In 1848 the Mexican province of Yucatan, which had more or less seceded from Mexico and declared itself neutral in the Mexican War, was facing a serious Indian uprising. It appealed, simultaneously, to the United States, Spain and England, offering "dominion and sovereignty" over itself to anybody who would help. Then, quite shrewdly, the agent of Yucatan pointed out, in Washington, that for either of the European countries to accept their offer would be a violation of the principles of Monroe. Polk sent the problem to the Senate. He did not exactly recommend annexation of Yucatan, but he did say that in the hands of a European power it would be dangerous to our security. He added that he had inside information that one of the foreign countries planned to accept Yucatan's offer.

This was the first time that an effort was made to twist the Monroe Doctrine to cover the intervention of the United States in the affairs of a neighbor state in order to prevent possible European intervention. It led to one of the most extensive debates on the Doctrine in Senate history. The opposition to the Doctrine—or, rather, to this interpretation of it—was led by John C. Calhoun, who had been in Monroe's Cabinet when the message was formulated.

From memory, Calhoun recalled the circumstances that

had prompted Monroe's speech. He maintained that it had been directed against the Holy Alliance and that, with the passing of that threat, the declarations of Monroe were no longer applicable. Also, according to Calhoun, the words in Monroe's speech were "declarations—nothing more. . . . Declarations are not policy, and cannot become settled policy. . . . The principle which lies at the bottom of his [Polk's] recommendations is that when any power on this continent becomes involved in internal warfare, and the weaker side chooses to make application to us for its support, we are bound to give them support or the offer of the sovereignty of the country may be made to some other country and accepted. It puts us in the power of other countries on this continent to make us a party to all their wars."

Calhoun's attack on the Doctrine was supported by all the Whigs in the Senate, although Calhoun, like Polk, was a Democrat. This extensive debate was the first occasion on which the Doctrine was treated as a political football, with disgruntled Whigs who disagreed with the Democrats' policy in the Mexican War associating the Doctrine with it in their consideration of the Yucatan question. When a change of government in Yucatan removed the Indian threat, the Senate resolution was withdrawn and the violent disagreement on the Doctrine died down, to be remembered only as the first attempt to use the Doctrine to justify United States intervention in Latin America, and the last strong attack on it as an expression of national policy.

From the inception of the Monroe Doctrine in 1823 until the 1860s the only diplomatic action on the part of the United States which might be termed an application of the

Doctrine was a treaty with Colombia in 1846. There was talk of an isthmian canal—there had been for many years. In asking the United States to guarantee Colombian sovereignty over any portion of their territory through which such a canal might pass, Colombia referred to the words of Monroe and Polk. The United States signed the treaty, although "most favored nation" commercial privileges in Colombia was undoubtedly a more compelling reason for making it than the Monroe Doctrine. And after making it, the United States suggested that Colombia seek similar guarantees from England and France.

Another treaty covering a proposed canal seemed to be, on the face of it, a complete violation of the Monroe Doctrine. This was the Clayton-Bulwer treaty with England, under which the two countries agreed to a joint protection of the projected canal and promised not to "occupy, fortify or colonize, or assume or exercise any dominion over Nicaragua, Costa Rica, the Mosquito Coast or any part of Central America." At the time there was no reference to the Doctrine in connection with this invitation to Great Britain to participate in Latin American affairs. It was considered that the treaty, rather than the Doctrine, would restrict her Central American expansion. Later, when the Doctrine had firmly entrenched itself in the American consciousness, the treaty would be loudly denounced as a pernicious entangling alliance that violated the sacred words of Monroe.

As the 1850s passed there was no further appeal to the Monroe Doctrine to oppose the anti-United States machinations of European diplomacy in Latin America. While public feeling for the Doctrine was growing at home, it was deteriorating in the states to the south. Expeditions of filibusters from the United States had much to do with the ill feeling south of the border. Most of these expeditions were actually outlaw raids bent on pillage and plunder rather than conquest. Some of them, like the Lopez raids on Cuba, involved disgruntled nationalists who operated from northern bases with private aid and financing. Many raids were broken up by alert Government action before they started, and none were supported or endorsed by the Government, but the Latin Americans were loathe to believe this, remembering, as they did, the sympathy of the United States toward the North Americans who had wrested Texas from Mexico and made it part of the northern republic.

The "king of the filibusters," and the man who did more more than any other to discredit the United States in the other Americas, was self-styled "General" William Walker. Before he started out to carve a kingdom in Central America, Walker had trained, successively, as a preacher, doctor, lawyer and editor. He was practising the latter profession in San Francisco when he was inspired, probably by an abortive filibustering expedition in Mexico stirred up by the French consul, to try his hand at conquering some territory to the south.

Walker's purpose was never entirely clear. He claimed that his first expedition was to protect the women and children on the Arizona border from Indian massacres. Also he was an ardent advocate of slavery, which he considered a "holy institution," and he dreamed of establishing a slave-holding empire to the south. Whatever his purpose, he set out in October, 1852, with forty-five men, landed on the extreme tip of Lower California, captured the town of La Paz, established a republic with himself as president and declared the people free of the tyranny of Mexico.

When he was reenforced by three hundred cutthroats from the north—mostly the unsuccessful scum of the California gold fields—he declared that the Mexican state of Sonora was also part of his republic, and started up the peninsula to invade it. By losses from desertion, Indian attacks and some Mexican resistance, his force was reduced to thirty-three men before he gave up and recrossed the border to surrender to the United States Army. He was tried for violating the neutrality laws and acquitted. Although the government tried to prosecute filibusters, it could never get a jury to convict one. Acquittals were usually followed by a public banquet in honor of the brigand.

Walker's next exploit was more far-reaching and, temporarily, more successful. There was, as usual, a revolution in progress in Nicaragua. Walker secured a contract from the "outs" to bring North Americans to Nicaragua, where they would receive grants of land and, as colonists, be liable for militia duty. With this quasi-legal document he openly sailed for the Central American republic in 1855 with fifty-seven men. He was promptly commissioned a colonel in the revolutionary army, and with his North Americans spearheading the native troops, he conquered Nicaragua in four months. A local man on the side for which he had been fighting was appointed provisional president. Walker then took his army over to the other side, with the understanding that they would nominate him for the presidency, and demanded an election. With his well-armed followers as poll watchers and, probably, vote counters, he won by a commanding majority.

He raised a new flag over his republic with a large five-pointed star and the motto "Five or None." To the four other Central American states, Costa Rica on the south and

Guatemala, El Salvador and Honduras on the north, the meaning of the motto was quite obvious. They all declared war against the interloper. With an army that never numbered more than thirty-five hundred Walker fought all four countries to a standstill. He undoubtedly would have put together his slave empire of five states if he had not run afoul of a man who was bigger than Central America—the North American financier, shipping and railroad magnate, Cornelius Vanderbilt.

Vanderbilt had made an exclusive contract with the old Nicaraguan government to transport pilgrims to the California gold fields across the country. He owned the ships that brought them down the Atlantic side, the boats that took them up the San Juan River and across Lake Nicaragua, the horses that carried them the twelve miles overland to the Pacific coast, and the ships that then took them to California. At the time, his Accessory Transit Company in Nicaragua was ferrying an average of two thousand gold seekers a month across the isthmus. It was supposed to pay Nicaragua $10,000 a year and ten percent of the profits, but claimed that there were no profits. Walker accused the company of keeping a double set of books and demanded $250,000. When this was not paid he seized the boats on the river and lake. Vanderbilt retaliated by stopping the service of the ocean steamers—Walker's only link with the outside world.

At the same time, two North American soldiers of fortune appeared to lead the troops of the Central American allies. Walker claimed that they were paid by Vanderbilt. Cut off from ammunition and reinforcements, he was soon penned up in a coastal village, besieged by the well-led allies. He surrendered to a United States man-of-war, was returned to New York to be cheered and fêted by a populace enthralled by his derring-do. Within a month he was back in Nicaragua at the head of one hundred and fifty North American recruits. He was well on his way to reconquering the country until the United States frigate *Wabash* put in an appearance, opened fire on Walker's camp and sent a landing force ashore to capture him. Back in Washington, Walker boldly put in a claim for damages caused by the *Wabash* to "his" country. The claim died in Congress, but President Buchanan sternly rebuked the captain of the *Wabash*, saying that he had set a dangerous precedent.

On Walker's third, and last, Central American invasion he was unable to reach Nicaragua because of patrolling United States and British warships. He landed in Honduras with one hundred men, and finding a revolution in progress, joined the "outs" and captured the seaport of Trujillo. Before he could proclaim another new republic a British warship appeared in the harbor and threatened to bombard the town unless he surrendered. He tried to escape up the coast, but when his force was laid low, almost to a man, by yellow fever, he was forced to surrender to a British landing force. They turned him over to the Hondurans, who promptly shot him.

There is nothing in the exploits of Walker and his fellow filibusters that connects directly with the Monroe Doctrine, except that this was the first instance in which there was a suspicion that "big business" was influencing United States foreign policy in Latin America. There were those who said that Vanderbilt had more to do with the action of the United States Navy in the matter than did the Secretary of State. And, more important, the actions of the filibusters supported, in the minds of Latin Americans, the growing idea that the United States was planning to take over the rest of the hemisphere. When returning filibusters were lionized by the press and public, and went unpunished by their government, Latin Americans could hardly be blamed for assuming that their actions were in accord with the purpose of their country. In the southern countries, a violent "Yankee go home" attitude started to take shape. A respected Chilean writer spoke for the more extreme Yankee haters when he said, in 1856:

Look at the empires which pretend to resuscitate the old idea of the domination of the globe: Russia and the United States. The first is very far away; the second is very near. Russia is limiting her warlike operations; the United States are extending theirs every day. . . . We already see fragments of America fall into the clutches of the Anglo-Saxon boa constrictor and involved in its coils. Yesterday Texas, after that northern Mexico and the Pacific salute a new lover. Today the advance guard of guerillas scour the isthmus. . . . We commence to follow the steps of the Colossus which steadily advances without fearing anyone; with its diplomacy, with its spreading cloud of adventurers; with its influence and its growing power. . . . We see that this nation, which had always been our star, menaces the autonomy of America. The Saxon of the north gathers his forces . . . to attain the possession of Olympus, which is the absolute dominion of America.

By 1860 the Monroe Doctrine was in ill repute in Latin America, rejected or ignored in Europe, condemned by vociferous Whigs at home. Only the man in the street had reverence for the message of Monroe, and he, even then, was not quite sure what it meant. In almost forty years the Doctrine had accomplished nothing. Of course, there had been no effective intervention by Europe in Latin America, but no one could prove that the Doctrine had anything to do with this. And, except for the Falkland Islands, there had been no further colonization in the Western Hemisphere. In 1860, by negotiation, Britain was induced to give up the Bay Islands, give the Mosquitoes back to Honduras and Nicaragua and declare Greytown a free port. No one claimed that this was done because of the Monroe Doctrine. But it is quite probable that Britain's realization of the growing weight of American public opinion was a factor in her decision to retreat. History cannot be written in terms of what might have been, but it is a fact that, whether because of, or in spite of, Monroe's words, the principle which he proclaimed had become a reality.

The First Big Challenge

For sixty years, until her death in 1927, a once beautiful woman lived in confinement in the Château de Bouchot, near Brussels. She was insane. Her reason had failed when her husband fell before a firing squad in Querétaro, Mexico. Born a Belgian princess, she had become an Austrian archduchess upon her marriage and then, briefly, a Mexican empress. Through the long years of her gentle captivity in the château, her broken mind dreamed that she was still the Empress Carlota and that she would soon join her husband, the Emperor Maximilian, when the troubles subsided in his far-off Mexican kingdom. In a way, the beautiful Carlota and the well-meaning but vacillating Maximilian were the most pathetic victims of the Monroe Doctrine.

The road to stable government in Mexico was a rocky one for more than a century after independence was gained from Spain in 1821. It started as a monarchy under the ruthless creole Emperor Agustín de Iturbide. The monarchy lasted only a year, and was the first of seventy-four governments that would try to rule the tortured country during the next fifty years: two empires, two regencies, and enough presidents and dictators to make up the balance. During the first hundred years there were approximately that number of revolutions—an average of one a year.

Relations between Mexico and the United States were never good. It was not easy to maintain good relations with a country in which the government sometimes changed from week to week, and where it was frequently difficult to determine which of two governments was *the* government. During the 1850s the relations between the neighboring states reached their lowest ebb. The Mexicans were far from satisfied with the "shotgun divorce" through which the United States had acquired California and New Mexico. They were convinced that the United States had an interest in acquiring more Mexican territory. And all of Europe agreed with them.

In 1853 Santa Anna, of Alamo infamy, came back into power, this time as a dictator—a self-styled "most serene highness" supported by the conservatives in the church, the army and among the large landowners. Santa Anna was never properly grateful to the United States. This country had brought him back from exile in Cuba in 1846 with the understanding that he would negotiate a settlement of the war between his country and the United States. He had promptly switched sides and put himself at the head of the Mexican forces. Even though Sam Houston had saved him from being lynched by irate Texans when he was captured at the battle of San Jacinto, he still disliked and distrusted his northern neighbors.

Santa Anna promptly sought the protection of Europe against what he termed the threatened aggression of the Colossus of the North. He first proposed to England, France and Spain a tripartite agreement to guarantee Mexican integrity. Then he sent an emissary to Europe to "enter into negotiations with the governments of London, Paris, Madrid and Vienna and make whatever offers were necessary to obtain from all these governments, or from any of them, the establishment of a monarchy derived from the dynastic houses of these powers." Nothing came of these appeals to Europe at that time. The attention of the foreign powers was centered on the war that had started in the Crimea. Queen Isabella of Spain expressed some interest in placing the Infante Don Juan of Bourbon on a Mexican throne, and some Spanish soldiers infiltrated the Mexican army, but a revolution in Spain nipped this project in the bud.

Although their governments did not act, most of the European diplomats in Mexico City did everything that they could to foster fear and distrust of the United States —particularly the French ambassador, who constantly appealed to the Quai d'Orsay for intervention in Mexico. "Only Europe can save Mexico," he said in one dispatch. And, in another, "Mexico has become the avowed object of the conquering ambition of the United States. If it finishes by falling into their hands it would be difficult to arrest the march of their domination in the New World. Masters of this immense territory, will they not be able to lay down the law to Europe?"

The American minister to Mexico, John Forsyth, was

acutely aware of the danger of foreign intervention. While the French minister was appealing for action from his country, Forsyth wrote to Washington:

It is not safe for statesmen of the United States to ignore the fact that other nations besides ours have their eager gaze fixed upon this rich and superb country. . . . If she cannot stand without the aid of some friendly power . . . what power . . . should occupy the commanding position of benefactor and friend? If the United States refuse, some one must. . . . Believe me, sir, we cannot afford to play "dog in the manger" with our Monroe Doctrine. Mexico cannot afford to perish for want of a medical interventor because we choose not to be the physician. She must lean upon some power. . . . If it be Europe, I can see a multitude of contingencies that will make Mexico the battleground for the maintenance of American supremacy in America; the theatre for the practical illustration of the value and the virtue of the Monroe Doctrine.

Back in Washington, there seemed to be more interest in getting a piece of Mexico than in Mexican independence. Sam Houston, now a Senator from Texas, introduced a resolution advocating a United States protectorate over Mexico and Central America and spoke for it heatedly with many references to the Monroe Doctrine. President James Buchanan proposed to Congress that the Mexican provinces of Sonora and Chihuahua be occupied, "for the better protection of the border." Neither of these proposals was acted upon by a Congress in which the members from the northern states looked upon the acquisition of added southern territory as a possible extension of slavery.

Meanwhile, there had been a succession of changes of government in Mexico that resulted, in 1858, in two governments—a conservative government in Mexico City and a liberal government under the Indian, President Juárez, at Vera Cruz. For three years they fought a bitter civil war, during which the United States recognized the Juárez government and loaned it four million dollars. Partly through this material aid, the Juárez government gained control of the country in January, 1861.

The civil war had left Mexico bankrupt. She had debts to Europe of eighty-two million dollars, plus fifteen million that France claimed, although Mexico had never received the money. During the war both sides had misappropriated the property of European nationals. The claims of European powers reached an astronomical sum. Juárez could not hope to pay. When he suspended interest payments on the national debt, England, Spain and France signed a convention for joint intervention in Mexico and landed on expeditionary force at Vera Cruz.

It soon became evident the Emperor Louis Napoleon of France had something more in mind than collecting real or fancied debts due his country. He was convinced that the United States had designs on Mexico. He was sure that only a strong Mexican government, tied closely to Europe, could maintain the "balance of power" in the New World. His beautiful, crafty, Spanish wife, allied with Mexican conservatives and clerics who had fled the liberal regime, pressed for the establishment of a monarchy.

Napoleon gave lofty reasons for his Mexican adventure. He said, "I seek nothing but good; convinced that to try to make a people prosperous is to work effectively for the prosperity of all." But to Marshal Forey, who led the French troops in Mexico, he wrote an enlightening explanation of his purpose. "We have no interest in seeing that republic [the United States] acquire the whole of the Gulf of Mexico, dominate from this vantage point the Antilles and South America, and become the sole dispenser of the products of the New World. Mistress of Mexico, and consequently of Central America and the passage between the two seas, there would be henceforth no other power in America than the United States. If, on the contrary, Mexico . . . maintains the integrity of its territory, if a stable government is constituted there by the arms of France, we shall have imposed an insuperable barrier to the encroachments of the United States, we shall have maintained the independence of our colonies in the Antilles . . . and this influence will radiate northward as well as southward, will create immense markets for our commerce and will procure the materials indispensable to our industry."

When the extent of Napoleon's plans became apparent, his allies pulled out. Great Britain promptly recalled its token force of seven hundred marines from Mexico. Spain, with trouble at home and dissension between her general in Mexico and the French leaders, withdrew more reluctantly. France landed thirty thousand additional troops who fought their way to Mexico City. Here the French minister hand-picked a Council of Notables from the Mexican conservatives. The Council promptly declared for monarchy and offered the crown to Archduke Ferdinand Maximilian of Austria, brother of Emperor Francis Joseph. That impractical, extravagant, well-meaning but deluded young man arrived in Mexico City on June 12, 1864, to mount a throne supported solely on French bayonets. He never really ruled all of Mexico. The Juárez government remained in existence, moving from place to place and fighting stubbornly and effectively with guerrilla tactics.

While all of this was going on in Mexico, even more momentous events were transpiring a few hundred miles north. When the European allies landed in Mexico in December of 1861, President Abraham Lincoln's administration was far more interested in the defense of Washington than the defense of Mexico. When Maximilian was crowned in June, 1864, the United States was more concerned with the Wilderness in Virginia than with the Halls of Montezuma. Throughout the years of the Civil War Lincoln's Secretary of State, William Seward, was forced to tread softly in his dealings with France. Obviously, the war-torn United States could not oppose France in Mexico with force. Also Seward could not go too far in endangering Franco-American relations at a time when the Confederacy was wooing France for aid and recognition. Considering that he had held only deuces, Seward played his cards masterfully for five years.

Seward had always been an ardent expansionist. As early as 1846 he had said, "Our population is destined to roll its resistless waves to the icy barriers of the North, and to encounter oriental civilization on the shores of the Pacific. The monarchs of Europe are to have no rest while they have a colony on this continent." In the 1860 campaign he had predicted that the "rapid decay" and "dissolution" of the governments of the Latin American states was the "preparatory stage for their reorganization as free, equal and self-governing members of the United States of America." His son said, in his biography, that one of his favorite topics of conversation was his desire to extend the United States "up to the pole and down to the tropics."

One of Seward's first acts on becoming Secretary of State was a proposal to prevent civil war by an aggressive foreign policy which would put the slavery issue into the background. This he expressed in the "Thoughts for the Consideration of the President" that he gave to Lincoln on April 1, 1861. He said, "I would demand explanations from Spain and France, categorically, at once. I would seek explanations from Great Britain and Russia and send agents into Canada, Mexico and Central America to rouse a vigorous continental spirit of independence on this continent against European intervention. And, if satisfactory explanations are not received from Spain and France, would convene Congress and declare war against them." He proposed to "smother a domestic insurrection" by a "war of conquest . . . supplant the slavery question by the Monroe Doctrine" and so change "a threatened dismemberment of the Union into the triumphant annexation of Canada, Mexico and the West Indies."

Fortunately, Abraham Lincoln was much too level-headed to pay attention to Seward's "Thoughts." And the Secretary's proposal to use the Monroe Doctrine to justify a policy of aggressive expansion was that of an opportunist. He had not been a strong Monroeist. As a freshman Whig Senator in 1853, Seward had not recognized the Doctrine as a continuing instrument of national policy. He said, "The principles involved have become a tradition among the American people, and on acknowledged occasions they would act upon them vigorously and with unanimity. On the other hand, the American people are a practical people, engrossed with actual business affairs and they will not act upon abstract principles, however approved, unless there is a necessity or at least an occasion. . . . The Monroe Doctrine was a right one—the policy was a right one . . . because it was well timed. It was a sagacious discovery of the tendency of the age. It will prevail if you affirm it. It will equally prevail if you neglect to affirm it hereafter as you have refused to do here-to-fore. As a practical question it has ceased to be. It is obsolete."

In 1861 Seward, as the international spokesman for a "practical people" who, counter to his opinion, were fighting with grim determination for "abstract principles," was faced with "an occasion" that called for the affirmation of the Doctrine that he called obsolete. For five years he kept steady, but polite, pressure on the French in terms of the Monroe Doctrine—without once mentioning the Doctrine by name.

He started in 1861 by acknowledging the rights of the allies to use force in Mexico for the correction of their real grievances. Such a right was never denied by the Monroe Doctrine. But, he added that he was sure that none of the allies would, "as a result or consequence of the hostilities to be inaugurated under the convention, exercise in the subsequent affairs of Mexico any influence of a character to impair the right of the Mexican people to choose and freely to constitute the form of its government."

By 1862 Napoleon's purpose was becoming increasingly clear. Seward's next move was to send a circular letter to United States ministers in Europe politely expressing President Lincoln's views on the subject of monarchy in America. "The President deems it his duty to express to the allies, in all candor and frankness, the opinion that no monarchial government which could be founded in Mexico ... would have any prospect of security or permanency. . . . In the President's opinion, the emancipation of this continent from European control has been the principal feature of its history during the last century. . . . The Senate of the United States has not, indeed, given its official sanction to the precise measures which the Presi-

dent has proposed for lending our aid to the existing government in Mexico. . . . This, however, is only a question
of domestic administration. It would be very erroneous to
regard such a disagreement as indicating any serious difference of opinion in this government or among the American
people in their cordial good wishes for the safety, welfare
and stability of the republican system of government in
that country."

Seward's language did not threaten, but a threat could
be read into his message—the President had in mind "precise measures" for lending aid to the Juárez government.
When the Maximilian Empire became a reality, Lincoln
himself spoke more bluntly. After Vicksburg he told Grant,
with Mexico in mind, "I am greatly impressed with re-
establishing the national authority in western Texas as
soon as possible." And to General Banks, "Recent events in
Mexico, I think, render early action in Texas more important than ever."

To a Senator who asked him, "Mr. President, how about
the French army in Mexico?" Lincoln replied with a char-
acteristically simple statement of the foreign policy that
Seward was pursuing on a wordy diplomatic plane. "I'm
not exactly 'skeered,' " he said, "but I don't like the looks
of the thing. Napoleon has taken advantage of our weak-
ness in our time of trouble, and has attempted to found a
monarchy on the soil of Mexico in utter disregard of the
Monroe Doctrine. My policy is, attend to one trouble at a
time. If we get well out of our present difficulties and restore the Union, I propose to notify Louis Napoleon that it
is about time to take his army out of Mexico. When that
army is gone, the Mexicans will take care of Maximilian."

It is obvious that Lincoln regarded the Monroe Doctrine

as a continuing instrument of the foreign policy of the United States. A plank in his platform for re-election in 1864 endorsed "the position taken by the government that the people of the United States can never regard with indifference the attempt of any European government to overthrow by force or to supplant by fraud the institutions of any Republican Government on the Western Continent." Wisely, he referred to the principle of the Monroe Doctrine as an expression of the will of the "people" of the United States—not a principle of any administration or party.

Lincoln agreed, although probably with some misgivings, to an effort to secure domestic peace by a union of the North and the South to enforce the Monroe Doctrine in Mexico. Old Francis Blair, Sr., although he held no position in the Government, was very influential politically. One of his sons was in the Cabinet. Another was a Union Corps Commander. He had ambitions to arrange a peace, and a great idea as to how it could be done. He wrote to his crony Horace Greeley that he had a scheme that was "benevolent as well as radical" and said, "I think I will hint it to Mr. Lincoln." As a result of the hint, Lincoln gave him a card on which he wrote, "Allow the bearer, F. P. Blair, Sr. to pass our lines, go South, and return. A. Lincoln."

Blair wrote to Jefferson Davis, an old friend from prewar days, that he wanted to come to Richmond to seek some title papers that might have been taken from his home while the Confederates were in possession of his property. With this he enclosed another note, saying that the first letter was only a front in case any questions were asked as to why he was in Richmond. Actually he had a much more important purpose in coming.

After dinner at the Confederate executive mansion, Blair and the Southern President went alone to the latter's study and Blair gave Davis a paper to read which described his plan in somewhat vague terms and weasel evasions. Carl Sandburg interprets Blair's proposal in simple terms as follows:

You can all come back into the United States any time that you are ready to take the Lincoln oath that you are back. . . . Go ahead now and put the Negroes into your armies and slavery will be at an end. Then if the North and South want peace nothing but soldiers from foreign countries can stop peace. If any states that went out of the Union should try to stay out on account of slavery, the only way they could do it would be by getting foreign armies to help them. That would mean some king or emperor across the ocean was running them. Can you think that people anywhere would stand for it? In this connection, look at Mexico. There the French Emperor Louis Napoleon has put an Austrian Archduke, Maximilian, on the throne and made a republic into a monarchy. There the grand old Monroe Doctrine, that Europe must keep their hands off this half of the earth, has been knocked into a cocked hat and kicked to pieces, and the North and South have done nothing about it. Why can't we get together on this? Why not drop this war of brothers, and the two of us, North and South, join what we've got and go down and throw Louis Napoleon's puppet off the throne and set up the Mexican republic again and get back our self-respect and put the Monroe Doctrine in operation again? Who would be the one man to head those armies for this cleanout in Mexico? Why, Jefferson Davis.

Blair went on to say that the Mexican minister at Washington had assured him that Juárez would be willing to step aside so that Jefferson Davis could be dictator of Mexico. He then warmed to his subject and assured Davis that by expelling European despotism from our southern flank he would "ally his name with those of Washington and Jackson. . . . If in delivering Mexico he should model its states in form and principle to adapt them to our Union and add a new Southern constellation to its benignant sky while rounding off our possessions on the continent at the Isthmus, and opening the way to blending the waters of the Atlantic and Pacific, thus embracing our republic in the arms of the ocean, he would complete the work of Jefferson."

It is most unlikely that Blair's "hint" to Lincoln exposed the aspects of the plan relating to Davis being the dictator of Mexico, or the annexation of Mexico to the United States. Davis gave Blair a letter to Lincoln which merely said that he was willing to "enter into negotiations for the restoration of peace." Back in Washington, Lincoln gave Blair a letter to Davis saying that he was, too. Blair went back to Richmond and made lengthy excuses about the Mexican offer. Obviously, Lincoln had told him that he would have no part of it. And so ended this most unusual effort to apply the Monroe Doctrine to settle the Civil War.

Immediately after Appomattox there was mounting public sentiment for the application of the Monroe Doctrine to the situation in Mexico. Individual congressmen and an almost united press demanded action. A steady stream of discharged soldiers filed through the Mexican embassy in Washington to inquire how they could enlist in the forces of Juárez. General Grant attended a Cabinet meeting to propose military action and secured from President Johnson a leave of absence for General Schofield so that this warrior could lead an independent United States force against Maximilian's French. General Phil Sheridan, commanding on the border, was told to give Schofield material support and to discharge any men who wanted to volunteer to go with him.

Seward, who had trod a narrow path with the French so long and so well, was convinced that the matter could be settled without recourse to arms. He cleverly sidetracked the fiery Schofield by flattering him into taking a special diplomatic assignment to France, saying, according to Schofield, "I want you to get your legs under Napoleon's mahogany and tell him he must get out of Mexico." The general never reached Napoleon. While he was entertained by minor diplomats in Paris, Seward used the growing restiveness of public opinion to put increased pressure on France. In a series of communications he hammered on the theme that the American people would not accept the principle "that a new European monarchial system can and ought to be permanently established on the American continent and in territory bordering on this republic."

By September of 1865 Seward felt strong enough to express this idea—that the people and the Congress could no longer be restrained—in the form of a veiled ultimatum, saying, "It may reasonably be anticipated that henceforth the Congress of the United States and the people in their primary assemblies will give a very large share of attention to . . . our relations toward France with regard to Mexico. Nor does it seem unwise to take into consideration that the presence of the military forces of the two nations, sometimes confronting each other across the border, has a tendency which both of them may regret to produce irritation and annoyance. . . . A time seems to have come when both nations may well consider whether the permanent interests of international peace and friendship do not require the exercise of a thoughtful and serious attention to the political questions to which I have thus adverted."

France, at first, expressed indignation at Seward's sterner tone. They would not be bullied by "haughty injunctions or threatening insinuations." Then, as Seward kept the pressure on and Sheridan kept 50,000 troops on the border, the Quai d'Orsay decided that they were "ready to engage in a frank exchange of views with the American government." They first tried to bargain, suggesting that they would withdraw French troops if the United States would recognize Maximilian's Government. Seward replied by repeating that the people of the United States would never accept a monarchy as a next-door neighbor. France then proposed to withdraw her troops and make a favorable commercial treaty if the United States would recognize her puppet. Seward instructed the American ambassador in Paris, John Bigelow, to remind the French that Congress was about to go into session, that the lawmakers were very concerned about the situation in Mexico, and that they were empowered by the Constitution to "direct by law the action of the United States in regard to that important subject." In other words, Congress could, and might, declare war.

Napoleon backed down. On Christmas Eve, 1865, he told Bigelow that he expected all French troops to be out of Mexico by the following autumn. Later, the French set up, and held to, a definite plan of withdrawal in three steps that left Maximilian deserted by 1867. As Lincoln had predicted, as soon as the French troops were gone, the Mexicans took care of Maximilian. Carlota went to Europe to plead, unsuccessfully, with Napoleon and the Pope for aid.

Maximilian refused to flee. With a handful of personal followers he fought on until he was betrayed to the Juárez forces and a Mexican firing squad.

As with almost every other aspect of the Monroe Doctrine, there are two schools of thought as to the part that it played in re-establishing a native government in Mexico. The more rabid proponents of the Doctrine claim that it was solely French fear of the mighty message of Monroe that drove them from Mexico. Extremists among its detractors maintain that the Doctrine had little or no bearing upon Napoleon's decision to withdraw. They ascribe his action to French public opinion, the cost of the Mexican adventure and the unsettled condition of affairs in Europe which necessitated the return of the troops.

Neither view is entirely correct, but it is probable that the attitude of the United States, and its seeming intention to enforce its point of view when the internal war ended, was by far the most important factor in Napoleon's decision to get out of the Western Hemisphere. With 400,000 Frenchmen under arms, he had no real need for the 28,000 troops in Mexico. It did cost money to keep them there, but for four years he had considered the cost worthwhile in terms of future commercial advantages. And although French public opinion was becoming increasingly opposed to the Mexican adventure, Napoleon's first moves at conciliation were made when the Assembly was not in session and would not be for five months—a period when the voice of the people had no immediate organ of expression. Also, all of these factors existed before the end of the Civil War, yet Napoleon made no move to bargain for United States recognition until Seward became more insistent after the war was over.

Those who maintain that the French withdrawal, as soon as the United States was in a position to put teeth into its Doctrine, was merely a coincidence, have to seek other explanations for the coincidental withdrawal of the Spanish from Santo Domingo.

During the 1850s there had been the usual unrest on that Caribbean island. In 1849 one of the more barbaric and colorful presidents of the Republic of Haiti, on the western end of the island, decided that he was an emperor, Faustin the First, and that he would conquer the Dominican Republic on the eastern end of the island. The Dominicans first appealed to France to establish a protectorate over their country. When the French ignored them they started to shop around, offering sovereignty over their country to any big brother who would protect them. Faustin's aggression was finally curbed by a threat of joint force on the part of France and England, but the Dominicans continued to seek a strong supporter, and toward the end of the decade, their hopes settled on Spain.

Spain was not reluctant to have her old colony back, but she did not feel strong enough to tangle with the United States, and her minister, Marshal O'Donnell, was very conscious of the Monroe Doctrine. In December, 1860, he said that regaining Spanish influence in the Western Hemisphere was very important but that action in Santo Domingo should wait on events in the United States. "The reunion of Santo Domingo brought about in such a manner as would give rise to suspicions . . . would not only turn the gaze of the terrified states of Latin America towards the United States, thus destroying the basis of our policy in America, the unity of our race, but also perhaps making the contending parties in America forget their internal discords, might lead them to group themselves under the Monroe Doctrine, a principle accepted without reserve by the slave states no less than by those where free labor prevails."

In March, 1861 the President of Santo Domingo, General Pedro Santana, made a deal with the Spanish Governor General of Cuba, General Francisco Serrano, independent of the Madrid government. Santana proclaimed that Santo Domingo had been annexed by Spain. Serrano sent Spanish troops from Cuba. When news of this *fait accompli* reached Madrid, O'Donnell issued a decree that the eastern half of the Caribbean island was again a Spanish possession. He did this one month after the bombardment of Fort Sumter.

When this happened, Seward had but recently taken office as Secretary of State. He was still in the aggressive, expansionist mood expressed in the "Thoughts" that he gave to Lincoln. Also, Spain had already accorded the status of a belligerent to the Confederacy, and an unfriendly Spain was not such a fearsome prospect as an unfriendly France. He did not deal with Spain with velvet gloves. Instead, he ordered the United States chargé in Madrid, Horatio Perry, to lodge a vigorous protest against the annexation, based squarely on its violation of the Monroe Doctrine. This was the most explicit and aggressive application of the Doctrine that had ever been presented to a foreign government. The note said, in part:

The Government of Her Most Catholic Majesty was not ignorant of the settled policy of the United States well known to all nations having any interest in the Western Hemisphere. It was precisely in reference to the possible future of the Republics formed from the ancient colonies of Spain in America that this policy was first announced by President Monroe in

1823 and has since been strictly adhered to by the United States and respected by Europe. . . .

We were the first and the most considerable of the American Republics. It became us therefore to take resolute ground against the projects then attributed to the Allied Powers, and to say to the nations of Europe with all respect, but with firmness and dignity, that we should not see with indifference the condition of things thus established changed or put in peril by the intervention of any monarchical or aristocatic government. We would not permit any new colony to be planted by Europe in America; though with such as already existed and had not obtained their independence we had no intention to interfere. . . . The political systems of the two continents had come to be radically distinct, and while we would ourselves refrain from all interference with the governments of Europe, reciprocally we claimed the right to say we would not suffer patiently the intervention of any European power in the internal affairs of the nations of America. . . .

The material interest of the United States in the change which has been attempted in the island of Santo Domingo is as small as it could well be. Perhaps in no other part of America would the overthrow of a republican government and the substitution of the power of a European state in its stead really affect the interests of the United States so little as the introducion of the Spanish jurisdiction in the island of Santo Domingo.

It is the moral and political significance of the act of Spain which gives it importance, and because this is the first instance since the foreign policy of the United States was announced to the Allied Powers of Europe in 1823 that any nation has failed to see its own clear interests in the maintenance of that policy on the one side and on the other. Spain alone and for the first time has chosen not to respect it. . . .

Filled with profound regret at this unhappy state of affairs, the undersigned has now to fulfill the duty imposed upon him by the President, and in the name of the government of the United States of America solemnly protests against the assumption or exercise of Spanish authority in the island of Santo Domingo; and this protest the United States in every case will expect to maintain.

This blustering dispatch was more notable for its high tone—and highhanded attitude—than for its accuracy. During the years since 1823 the policy announced by Monroe had not been "strictly adhered to by the United States," and it had never been "respected by Europe." But the communication made it clear that the Doctrine which Seward had called obsolete was now the basis of his foreign policy.

These words were fighting words, issued at a time when the United States was girding to fight—but not with Spain. In the words of the diplomat, the President might "expect to maintain" a protest to Spain, but, at the time, he had no means of doing so. The armies of North America were aligned against each other. Spain realized this. The Spanish minister returned a contemptuous reply to Perry's note, saying that this was the first time that the Spanish Government had ever been officially advised of the existence of the Monroe Doctrine and that "The government of the Queen neither accepts or declines this policy. It limits itself to saying that it does not think this an opportune time to discuss it." The reply went on to make the point that it was the Dominicans themselves who had decided that they wanted to be governed by Spain. Did the United States, which so fervently supported the right of the people to determine their form of government, propose to deny this right to the people of Santo Domingo?

This point was difficult to refute, although it was not valid. It was Santana who had brought about the Spanish annexation to support his crumbling power. The people of

Santo Domingo showed their attitude by putting up such a stiff resistance to foreign rule that Spain soon had 25,000 troops fighting Dominican guerrillas.

In 1861 Seward had no choice but to back down with as much dignity as possible—which was not much. In reply to a direct question as to whether the United States meant to threaten Spain he replied that "the United States was not accustomed to utter threats, and it belonged to Congress alone to take action." He added that Congress, at the moment, was too busy with other matters to concern itself with Santo Domingo. Then Seward lapsed into a sullen silence until the domestic war situation seemed to warrant a reiteration of the attitude of the United States toward foreign intervention.

The occasion for this took place in May, 1864. As a result of a trifling incident in Peru, an officious Spanish diplomat and an aggressive Spanish admiral seized some islands off the coast of that country, using the interesting excuse that Spain had never recognized the independence of Peru. Seward, put in a stronger position by the current successes of Union arms, immediately instructed the Ambassador at Madrid to "make it known to Her Catholic Majesty that the United States cannot yield their assent to the positions thus assumed in the name of Spain; or regard with indifference an attempt to reduce Peru by conquest and re-annex its territory to the Kingdom of Spain."

Seward went on to refer to the French in Mexico and the Spanish in Santo Domingo, saying that the Latin American states were fearful that the European powers which had once held them as colonies were planning to again place them in that condition. He then played the theme of his favorite tune in dealing with the French—the growing

demand for action on the part of the people of the United
States. He said, "These apprehensions are not unlikely to
be entertained by the whole people of the United States.
The proceedings in Spain gives them a color which is to be
deeply regretted. Indeed, a general discontent with the
forbearance of the government is already manifest. Should
the sentiment of this country demand a reconsideration of
the policy of neutrality which this government has hitherto
maintained, it is much to be feared that new complications
might arise which would . . . endanger the general peace of
nations."

The seizure of the Peruvian islands had not been authorized by the Spanish Government, and it immediately
repudiated the action. But the answer to Seward's blast was
interesting. The Spanish Foreign Secretary assured the
United States minister "that the Monroe Doctrine of the
United States would not be called in question by any proceeding of Spain in or against Peru. If President Monroe
were alive and on the spot he would see nothing running
counter to his famous declaration." Shortly before Bull
Run Spain had never "officially" heard of the Monroe Doctrine. Shortly before Appomattox they seemed to be quite
concerned about it.

The Spanish gave up Santo Domingo and withdrew their
troops in January, 1865. They did not do this wholly in
deference to the opinion of the United States; Spanish poverty, Spanish public opinion and yellow fever, which had
decimated half of their troops, probably had more to do
with it than the Monroe Doctrine. But again, as with
France in Mexico, it seems more than a coincidence that it
was done just at the time when the people of the United
States were starting to become aroused at the violations of

their sacred Doctrine—and when the Colossus of the North had the muscle to enforce it.

The actions of Spain and, particularly, France during the Civil War were the first great challenge to the Monroe Doctrine. The challenge was met—decisively. From that time, although the Doctrine might be condemned, reviled, belittled and repudiated by the chancelleries of Europe, it was never again ignored or directly challenged—until 1962.

In the United States, public opinion toward it as a sort of holy dogma had started to consolidate. A new nationalistic spirit would grow out of the civil conflict of the 1860s, and an increasing faith in the message of Monroe—however it was interpreted—would be an expression of that spirit.

Up to this time, Monroe's basic principles had not been perverted in practice, although there had been those who tried to twist them to support United States "manifest destiny" and aggressive expansion. But Seward described, in 1866, the Doctrine as it was then understood—a Doctrine that did not depart from the message of Monroe or the restatement of Polk.

The policy of the United States in regard to the several Spanish-American states is, or ought to be, well known now, after the exposition it has received during the last five years. We avoid in all cases giving encouragement to expectations which, in the varying course of events, we might find ourselves unable to fulfill; and we desire to be known as doing more than we promise rather than falling short of our engagements. On the other hand, we maintain and insist, with all the decision and energy which is compatible with our existing neutrality, that the republican system which is accepted by the people of any one of those states shall not be wantonly assailed. . . . We thus give to those republics the moral support of a sincere, liberal and, as we think it will appear, a useful friendship.

5

The Golden Age of the Doctrine

During the last half of the nineteenth century the armies of Europe were almost constantly on the march to create colonial empires. Practically all of Africa was divided up among the Europeans. Much of Asia fell into occidental hands. Britain took India. By the end of the century everybody was grabbing chunks of China. Everywhere weak nations were losing their independence to the modern military powers of Europe—everywhere, that is, except in the Western Hemisphere.

Ardent Monroeists have made much of this. They credit the Doctrine with preventing the weak states of Latin America from sharing the fate of those of Asia and Africa. Detractors of the Doctrine say that the attitude of the United States had little or nothing to do with it. They maintain that European powers kept "hands off" the Western Hemisphere because they were too busy elsewhere, and that many of the Latin American states were quite capable of defending themselves.

We will never know what might have happened had there been no Monroe Doctrine. We do know what did happen. There was no definite effort on the part of a European power to acquire dominion over any Latin American state. But there were a great many rumors of projected activity in this direction. American diplomats were never so busy brandishing the Monroe Doctrine as they were in the thirty-five years following the Civil War. In the Caribbean area alone the Doctrine was held up as a shield against real or fancied danger from across the sea at least twenty-five times.

It seems reasonable to assume that the Doctrine had some effect in maintaining the integrity of the hemisphere during this period. Although some of the larger Latin states could have taken care of themselves against anything short of a major military effort, most of them, particularly in and around the Caribbean area, could have been brought under European influence with little more than a corporal's guard. Witness Walker's conquest of Nicaragua with fifty-seven men.

There were some instances where it was obvious that Uncle Sam's Doctrine was influential in the foreign offices of Europe. When Haiti made one of its perennial moves to secure European support for a dying government by offering the Môle St. Nicolas to France as a naval base, France referred to the Doctrine as a reason for declining. A French minister told the United States minister, "We are far from seeking in the New World advantages of any sort which might expose us to confront the redoubtable Monroe Doctrine. I do not personally believe in the liberality, wisdom and force of this doctrine ... which tends to maintain the nations of the world apart instead of bringing them closer to each other ... but be this as it may, you shall not have, this time at least, an occasion to apply it to us."

Most of the applications of the Doctrine during this period concerned very minor matters, and it is probable that it was brandished at spooks more often than at living threats. After the Civil War the United States started to "feel its oats" as a world power. Its diplomats were very conscious of its dignity and position. And suspicion of European motives was easily aroused. Both statesmen and the public remembered the recent French and Spanish exploits in the Western Hemisphere at a time when the United States was not in a position to intervene.

During the administration of President Grant the Doctrine was expanded by what has been termed the "No transfer" principle. Although the basic idea was not new, it received definite form through two messages which Grant sent to the Congress. The first of these related to a revolution in Cuba against the rule of Spain. No foreign nation was actually involved in the dispute, but Grant seemed to think that Spain might decide to get out of the costly campaign by selling the island. In 1869 he told Congress:

The United States have no disposition to interfere with the existing relations of Spain to her colonial possessions on this continent. They believe that in due time Spain and other European powers will find their interests in terminating those relations and establishing their present dependencies as independent powers—members of the family of nations. These dependencies are no longer regarded as subject to transfer from one European power to another. When the present relation of colonies ceases, they are to become independent powers, exercising the right of choice and self-control in the determination of their future conditions and relations with other powers.

The next year, 1870, Grant took the "no transfer" principle one step further. This time the Dominican Republic sparked the message. Grant claimed that he had information that Germany was trying to buy Samaná Bay, in Santo Domingo, as a naval base. In this connection he said, "The Doctrine promulgated by President Monroe has been adhered to by all political parties and I now deem it proper to assert the equally important principle that hereafter no territory on this continent shall be regarded as subject of transfer to a European power."

This aspect of the "no transfer" principle went a long way beyond Monroe. The earlier President had taken a position against any European power trying to reconquer an independent state, or establishing a new colony in the Western Hemisphere. Grant now said that two European states could not make an agreement covering the colonial possession of one of them, and that no Latin American nation could, of its own free will, become sovereign to a European power.

On the face of it this seemed to be a rather violent interference with the rights of the sovereign states of Latin America. Spain had brought up this principle in connection with her annexation of Santo Domingo. In that case it had not been valid because the "voluntary" transfer of sovereignty had been made by a corrupt government—it was not the will of the people. But if the people of a Latin American state decided, in an orderly manner, that they wanted to align themselves with a country across the sea, did the United States have any right to deny them this privilege? An analogy might be made by assuming that Alaska, as an independent state, wanted to join the United States but was prevented from doing so by its big neighbor, Russia.

But the people accepted Grant's expansion of the Doctrine without question. Obviously what he said related to the basic reason for Monroe's message—an occasion on which "our rights are invaded or seriously menaced." The acquisition of neighboring territory by a strong foreign power, in any manner whatsoever, might very possibly menace the United States. It should be noted that, in both messages, Grant referred to "this continent" rather than "this hemisphere." He did not make it explicit as to whether the principle applied beyond Central America and the Caribbean area.

Throughout the 1870s, 80s and early 90s the State Department and its ministers abroad were keenly sensitive to the possible encroachment of European nations in the Caribbean area through a transfer of territory. The acquisition of the Danish West Indies—now the Virgin Islands—by some other country was a constant fear. Seward had wanted to buy the islands in 1867, but Congress would not approve. A succession of secretaries of state were convinced that somebody else was about to buy them, and on seven different occasions the Monroe Doctrine was brandished to warn off Germany, France and England.

The two republics on the island of Santo Domingo were also frequent targets in defense of which the Monroe shield was raised. Their petty presidents and dictators were always on the lookout for a "deal" with a European country through which they could personally profit. The Môle St.

Nicolas in Haiti and Samaná Bay in the Dominican Republic were ideal for naval bases. Eight warnings were issued to Germany, France and England on this subject. Puerto Rico, Dutch Curaçao, the Bay Islands of Honduras and the Island of Tortuga were also sensitive spots to which the Monroe Doctrine was applied, either directly or by implication, to thwart a fancied threat of transfer.

Actually, there is no record that any foreign power had designs on this area. All of the instances in which the Doctrine was brandished were based on rumors, which were vehemently denied in London, Paris and Berlin. No one can tell what might have happened if the diplomats of Downing Street, the Quai d'Orsay and the Wilhelmstrasse had not known how strongly the man in the street in the United States felt about the Doctrine.

As in almost every other period there was a violation of the Doctrine which the United States did nothing about. In 1870 Sweden offered to sell the Island of St. Bartholomew to the United States, saying that Italy wanted to buy it but the United States was offered first refusal. Secretary of State Hamilton Fish replied that Congress would not approve the purchase, but that a sale to Italy "might be construed as adverse to that cardinal policy of the United States which objects to new colonies of European governments in this hemisphere."

Sweden did not sell to Italy, but, seven years later, she sold the island to France without consulting the United States. When the United States minister at Stockholm was advised of it, two weeks after the deed was done, he expressed "dissatisfaction." Sweden replied that she had acquired the island from France before the Monroe Doctrine came into existence and was merely returning it to its original owner. This is another of numerous instances, like the Falkland Islands, in which the practical threat to the United States, rather than the principle involved, was the basis for the application, or lack of application, of the Doctrine. Ownership of a dot of land with a population of less than three thousand could not in any way jeopardize the interests of the United States.

During all of this period there were many cases in which foreign powers used force, or the threat of force, against Latin American states without arousing the ire or interest of Washington. In Haiti alone, at seven different times, France, Germany, England, Spain and Russia used or threatened strong-arm methods with the black politicians of that unruly republic. These were instances in which the European countries had just grievances—the collection of debts or the protection of nationals. The position of the United States was that the Monroe Doctrine did not prohibit foreign powers from using force or waging war in the Western Hemisphere for just cause—so long as they had no territorial or political ambitions.

The Doctrine took a long step forward in the eyes of the world in 1895, when it was applied to settle a boundary dispute between Great Britain and Venezuela. This dispute had started as far back as 1840 when a British geographer surveyed a line between British Guiana and Venezuela which was very favorable to the former. Venezuela protested. Britain offered to compromise. Venezuela refused. Finally, both countries agreed to leave the jungle territory as a sort of "no man's land," and so it remained until 1875, when the subject was brought to life again by the discovery of gold in the disputed territory. There was much haggling for eleven years until the countries broke diplomatic relations.

During this period, Venezuela made frequent appeals to Washington in terms of the Monroe Doctrine, without effect. In the main, the South Americans were told that the North Americans were sympathetic, that "this government could not look with indifference to the forcible acquisition of such territory by Great Britain," and "the moral position of the United States in these matters is well known through the enunciation of the Monroe Doctrine." Toward the end the United States politely offered to arbitrate. Neither side accepted the offer and nothing else was done.

In 1894 Venezuela hired a former United States minister to Caracas as a "special agent" in the United States—in fact, a propagandist. This gentleman published, and widely distributed, a booklet entitled *British Aggressions in Venezuela, or the Monroe Doctrine on Trial*. Also, he talked to his Congressman, Leonidas Livingston of Georgia, and induced him to introduce a resolution in the House calling on both parties to arbitrate. Livingston said that, if the United States did not take some action under the Monroe Doctrine it would be "such a surrender of national prestige as would make us the jest of the civilized world." Livingston's resolution was passed unanimously by both Houses of Congress.

The public and the press were more aggressive than the Congress in their demand for action. Said the *Atlanta Constitution:* "We need a revival of Americanism and the unmistakable assertion of the Monroe Doctrine." From the *New York Telegram:* "England, France and Germany may yet have to be diplomatically informed that the Monroe

Doctrine has never been abrogated." The *Chicago Tribune* said, "The United States under the Monroe Doctrine could never look on complacently at such an absorption of Venezuelan territory." These were typical of almost every headline across the nation.

Senator Henry Cabot Lodge summed up the national attitude by saying, "All that England has done has been a direct violation of the Monroe Doctrine, and she has increased and quickened her aggressions in proportion as the United States has appeared indifferent. The time has come for decisive action. The United States must either maintain the Monroe Doctrine and treat its infringement as an act of hostility, or abandon it. . . . But the American people are not ready to abandon the Monroe Doctrine, or give up their rightful supremacy in the Western Hemisphere. On the contrary, they are ready now to fight to maintain both. . . . The supremacy of the Monroe Doctrine should be established, and at once—peaceably if we can, forcibly if we must."

The interesting aspect of the public attitude in connection with the Venezuelan dispute is that the people were willing to risk war solely for the preservation of the precious Doctrine. Certainly there was no threat to American interests in the ownership of a few thousand square miles of jungle in South America. In most instances when the Doctrine had previously been applied its application was justified by a real or imagined infringement on American security. But now the Doctrine had reached the point where it was worth fighting for purely as a matter of principle.

President Grover Cleveland was not one to ignore public opinion, nor was his new, belligerent Secretary of State,

Richard Olney. With Cleveland's approval, Olney sent to Great Britain, not a request, but a demand that England submit the dispute to arbitration. This 12,000-word document is one of the most unusual in the diplomatic history of the United States. It started by reviewing the history of the dispute in a way that indicated that the United States was entirely on the side of Venezuela. This section concluded with the statement that "The government of the United States has made it clear to Great Britain and to the world that the controversy is one in which both its honor and its interests are involved and the continuance of which it cannot regard with indifference."

The document then outlined the history of the Monroe Doctrine, in connection with which Mr. Olney was a better partisan than a historian. He said that the Doctrine was "the controlling factor in the emancipation of South America," and to it "the independent states which now divide that region between them are largely indebted for their existence." He also said that, from the inception of the Doctrine, Great Britain had given it "an open and unqualified adhesion that has never been withdrawn." This was surely news to the British Foreign Office.

Olney spent few words in relating the boundary dispute to the Monroe Doctrine. He merely said that it was "in any view far within the scope and spirit of the rule as uniformly accepted and acted upon." This was obviously ridiculous. The Doctrine as a whole had never been uniformly accepted outside the United States, and it had never been acted upon in a similar situation in the past.

Most of Olney's document had little bearing upon the case in hand. Rather, it seemed to question the right of any European countries to have American possessions by saying that they were "unnatural and inexpedient." This, presumably, applied to Canada, to Cuba and to all of the colonial possessions of France, England, Holland and Spain which had existed long before the time of Monroe's message, and which the Doctrine promised to respect.

Not content with offending England, Olney went on to usurp authority over his Latin American neighbors by saying, "Today, the United States is practically sovereign on this continent, and its fiat is law upon the subjects to which it confines its interposition." This, he explained, with some obnoxious moralizing and bragging, was "not simply by reason of its high character as a civilized state, nor because wisdom and justice and equity are the invariable characteristics of the United States. It is because, in addition to all other grounds, its infinite resources combined with its isolated position render it master of the situation and practically invulnerable as against any or all other powers."

The entire tone of Olney's message was that of a domestic political speech. As a diplomatic document it was unclear, verbose, belligerent and ill-mannered. On the whole, it was an insult to a friendly nation. The end of it was somewhat more moderate, although it demanded rather than urged arbitration with the statement that, if a satisfactory answer was not forthcoming, promptly, the President would have to lay the matter before Congress.

Lord Salisbury, Britain's Foreign Secretary, was a cold, old-line diplomat who was not easily moved by blustering threats. When he received the document, on July 20, 1895, he merely said that it would have to be discussed with Her Majesty's legal officers. Then he pigeonholed it for four months, and when he finally did reply, the answer was sent by mail instead of cable.

In his answer he first said that the Monroe Doctrine had nothing to do with the matter under consideration, which was "simply the determination of the frontier of a British possession which belonged to the throne of England long before the Republic of Venezuela came into existence." He presented some arguments to show why the Monroe Doctrine did not apply. Then, he went further by saying, "In the remarks which I have made I have argued on the theory that the Monroe Doctrine itself is sound. I must not, however, be understood as expressing any acceptance of it on the part of Her Majesty's government. It must always be mentioned with respect, on account of the distinguished statesman to whom it is due, and the great nation who has generally adopted it. But international law is founded on the general consent of nations; and no statesman, however eminent, and no nation, however powerful are competent to insert into the code of international law a novel principle which was never recognized before, and which has not been since accepted by the government of any other country. . . . The government of the United States is not entitled to affirm as a universal proposition, with reference to a number of independent states for whose conduct it assumes no responsibility, that its interests are concerned in whatever may befall those states simply because they are situated in the Western Hemisphere."

Lord Salisbury's answer concluded with a firm refusal to arbitrate unless a large section of the disputed territory was first ceded to Great Britain without question.

The rather supercilious tone of the British answer, and the delay in delivering it, infuriated Grover Cleveland. He requested that Congress pass a resolution to the effect that if Great Britain did not agree to arbitration, the United

States would appoint a commission to decide the matter independently, and said that if England did not accept the findings of the committee, it would be "the duty of the United States to resist by every means in its power, as a willful aggression upon its rights and interests, the appropriation by Great Britain of any lands . . . which after investigation we have determined of right belongs to Venezuela."

Both Houses of Congress passed the resolution unanimously, without debate and with much flag-waving reference to the Monroe Doctrine. There was much excitement, little dignity, in the legislative chambers. Senators and Representatives stood in the aisles and cheered when the vote was taken. The press and the public echoed and exceeded the lawmakers' belligerency. Since the Mason-Slidell incident in the Civil War there had been no such crisis in Anglo-American relations. The United States was ready to go to war with England. The Venezuelan jungle was not the real issue. It is doubtful whether anybody in the United States really cared who owned it. But England had defied the Monroe Doctrine. In the mood that prevailed at the close of the eighteenth century, this was an insult that could not be tolerated.

England coaled up the fleet, but largely as a defensive measure. Fortunately, cooler heads prevailed on the other side of the Atlantic. Great Britain did not feel that her honor was at stake on the Venezuelan question. She had more pressing problems nearer home and the last thing she wanted was to become embroiled with the United States over an insignificant boundary dispute in South America. Lord Salisbury was instructed to back down.

Considering his lordship's initial comments on the Monroe Doctrine, his first move was somewhat unusual. He proposed an international conference on the Doctrine between the United States and all European countries having Latin American possessions. Great Britain would accept the decisions of this conference as to the meaning of the Doctrine in general and whether it applied to the Venezuelan dispute. In short, Britain was willing to accept the Monroe Doctrine if the United States would explain it and set forth the conditions under which it was applicable.

Cleveland, in his message to Congress, had claimed that the Doctrine was based on international law because a basic premise of the law of nations was the right of any country to take whatever action it considered advisable for its own defense, and any European encroachment in the Western Hemisphere would be a threat to the security of the United States. However, he wanted no part of having the Doctrine interpreted by international agreement. He instructed Olney to cable Salisbury that "The United States is content with the existing status of the Monroe Doctrine, which, as well as its application to said controversy, it regards as completely and satisfactorily accepted by the people of the Western Continents."

Olney then made a counter proposal to the effect that, in any arbitration, the occupancy of a portion of the disputed territory by British nationals for a period of sixty years should be given great weight as indicating English ownership. In other words, if the English were there at about the time that the Monroe Doctrine came into existence, it could be considered that they had a right to the territory. After haggling to get the time of residency reduced to fifty years, the English accepted arbitration by the United States. Although England received some of the disputed territory, the resulting agreement was, on the whole, favorable to Venezuela.

This trifling dispute over a few thousand square miles of jungle did much to enhance the international prestige of the United States and the Monroe Doctrine. The strongest power in Europe had accepted the principle that any territorial questions in the Americas would be settled by Americans. Every foreign office in Europe fumed—but a precedent had been established. A short time later France willingly submitted a boundary dispute between French Guiana and Brazil to arbitration.

In the United States, Venezuela had been forgotten by the time the arbitration was concluded, but the wave of patriotic pride in the Doctrine continued to crest. Perhaps the greatest beneficiary of the incident was the United States Navy. When it started, the Navy had been neglected since the end of the Civil War. It was suddenly realized that the Doctrine, if it had to be enforced, was no stronger than the Navy. The same Congress that rattled the sword at Britain passed a whopping naval appropriation bill—the beginning of the ascendency of the United States to the status of a first-rate naval power.

Before the dawn of the twentieth century another interpretation of the Monroe Doctrine occurred which, although of little moment at the time, would later contribute much to the confusion concerning it. On August 24, 1898, Tsar Nicholas II of Russia invited the nations of the world to a Peace Conference at The Hague, in Holland. Twenty-six nations, including the United States, attended.

Before the American delegation left they were instructed by Secretary of State John Hay to suggest the idea of establishing an international tribunal of arbitration to which "the contracting parties will agree to submit . . . questions of disagreement between them, excepting such as may relate to or involve their political independence or territorial integrity." It is difficult to see how the participation of the United States in such an agreement could possibly violate the Monroe Doctrine. The principles that were excepted—political independence and territorial integrity—were the only principles covered by the Doctrine.

Sitting in Holland, thinking about their instructions, the members of the United States delegation started to fear that maybe Hay's proposal would be a violation of the Doctrine. The leader of the delegation, Andrew White, wrote in his diary, "It is indeed, a question whether our people will be willing to have matters of difference between South American states, or between the United States and a South American state, or between European and South American states, submitted to an arbitration in which the majority of the judges are subjects of European powers." White cabled for, and was granted, more latitude in negotiating an arbitration agreement.

The agreement that was finally reached, entitled *The Convention for the Pacific Settlement of International Disputes,* was so innocuous as to be almost meaningless. Arbitration was not made obligatory. There would be a court of arbitration available to which the parties to a dispute could appeal if they so desired. France added an article which said that all of the signatory states should "consider it a duty" to remind the participants in a dispute that the court was there, but that was only to be considered as a friendly act.

For some reason that is difficult to fathom Admiral Mahan, another of the United States delegates, wondered

whether this French paragraph was "likely to be considered as an infringement of the Monroe Doctrine." His colleagues, knowing the touchy attitude toward the sacred
dogma back home, agreed with him. White wrote, "We
fear lest, when the convention comes up for ratification in
the Senate of the United States, some over-sensitive pa-
triot may seek to defeat it by insisting that it is really a
violation of time-honored American policy at home and
abroad—the policy of not entangling ourselves in the affairs
of foreign nations, on this side, and of not allowing them
to interfere in our affairs, on the other."

To correct this possible threat to the Monroe Doctrine,
the delegation penned a declaration which said: "Nothing
contained in this Convention shall be construed as to require the United States of America to depart from its traditional policy of not intruding upon, interfering with or
entangling itself in the political questions or policy of international administration of any foreign state; nor shall
anything in the said Convention be construed to imply a
relinquishment by the United States of its traditional attitude toward purely American questions."

White described the scene on the day of the signing.
After the secretary read the American declaration, "the
conference was asked whether anyone had any objection, or
anything to say regarding it. There was a pause of about a
minute, which seemed to me about an hour. Not a word
was said—in fact, there was dead silence—and so our declaration embodying a reservation in favor of the Monroe
Doctrine was duly recorded and became part of the proceedings."

This little, entirely unnecessary, declaration at the
Hague Conference was to thwart, in future years, many ef-

forts at intelligent treaty-making. It added a dimension to
the Monroe Doctrine in the eyes of the most ardent isolationists which made many international negotiations difficult. A case could be made to support the statement that,
twenty-five years later, the League of Nations was wrecked
on this declaration embodied in the Hague Convention. It
was born of the fears in the minds of the United States delegates that American public opinion would not accept any
agreement which in any way involved the United States
that did not contain a specific exception in favor of the
precious Doctrine. And, at that time, the fears of the delegates were probably well founded.

6

"Not So Far from Here—"

The above title is the opening line of a song that was popular during the Prohibition era in the United States. The place referred to was Cuba in which, the next line of the song proclaimed, "There's a very lively atmosphere." There has always been a lively atmosphere in Cuba, although the liveliness of Sloppy Joe's Bar, the great Havana tourist attraction during Prohibition, was very different from the liveliness of Fidel Castro.

It is not unreasonable to say that the United States has always had a Cuban problem—except when she had a Cuban crisis. And, through the years, the Monroe Doctrine has been very much involved in coping with the problem or crisis, although it has seldom been "invoked" or mentioned by name in diplomatic affairs relating to Cuba. It might be said that a Cuban problem contributed to Monroe's original message. A study of George Canning's correspondence at the time he proposed the joint action against the Holy Alliance shows that he was very concerned with the possibility of the United States taking Cuba. The agreement he proposed was, in part, to prevent this.

The importance of Cuba to the United States in the early days is obvious from a glance at a map of the Caribbean. From it, traffic in and out of the Gulf of Mexico could be controlled. For a long period the Mississippi was the only outlet for the western states of the Union, and whoever controlled Cuba could control the mouth of the Mississippi. A canal through the Central American isthmus would be virtually indefensible against a strong, unfriendly power in Cuba.

Most of the early statesmen realized this. Thomas Jefferson repeatedly expressed a desire to see Cuba annexed to the United States. In 1809, just before he went out of office, he said, "We must have the Floridas and Cuba." Later that same year he wrote to Madison to suggest that Napoleon, after his conquest of Spain, might be willing to give Cuba to the United States in return for an agreement that this country would not interfere with his plans elsewhere in Latin America. "That would be a price," said Jefferson, "and I would immediately erect a column on the southernmost limit of Cuba and inscribe on it a *ne plus ultra* as to us in that direction."

In April, 1823, seven months before Monroe's message, John Quincy Adams made a strong case for the acquisition of Cuba in a letter to the United States minister to Spain in which he said: "Cuba, almost in sight of our shores, from a multitude of considerations, had become an object of transcendent importance to the commercial and political interests of our Union. . . . In looking forward to the probable course of events, for the short period of half a century, it is scarcely possible to resist the conviction that the annexation of Cuba to our Federal Republic will be indispensable to the continuance and integrity of the Union itself. . . . Cuba, forcibly disjointed from its unnatural connection with Spain, and incapable of self-support, can gravitate only toward the North American Union, which . . . cannot cast her off from its bosom."

Jefferson, in his reply to Monroe's letter regarding Canning's proposal, pointed up both the desirability of incorporating Cuba into the United States or, if this was impractical, keeping it out of England's hands. He said that before accepting the idea of a joint statement against the designs of the Holy Alliance, "we have first to ask ourselves a question. Do we wish to acquire to our own confederacy any one or more of the Spanish provinces? I candidly confess that I have ever looked on Cuba as the most interesting addition that could ever be made to our system of states. The control which, with Florida point, this island would give us over the Gulf of Mexico and the countries and the isthmus bordering on it . . . would fill up the measure of our political well being. Yet, as I am sensible that this can never be obtained, even with her own consent, but by war; and its independence, which is our second interest (and especially its independence from England) can be secured without it, I have no hesitation in abandoning my first wish to future chances and accepting its independence with peace, and friendship with England, rather than its association at the expense of war and her enmity."

When Jefferson wrote this, in 1823, it was assumed that Cuba would, sooner or later, join the parade of mainland colonies that had revolted against Spanish rule. There were several reasons why she did not at the time of the mainland revolutions. Spain had been somewhat more liberal toward Cuba than toward the other provinces. She permitted greater latitude in matters of trade and did not make determined efforts to suppress the extensive and profitable smuggling with the United States. Also, slavery was a greater factor in Cuba than on the mainland. More than half the population of Cuba was black. White refugees to Cuba from neighboring Haiti had told of the horrors of the rebellion of the blacks. Potential leaders of a revolution in Cuba feared a black rebellion more than they disliked Spanish rule, and such a rebellion might well follow on the heels of freedom from Spain.

Until the 1860s United States diplomacy relating to Cuba was based on the fear that it would become subject to a stronger power than Spain, either through conquest or voluntary cession. The policies of England and France were motivated by the fear that it would be acquired by the United States. As early as 1822 Adams became suspicious that England had a nefarious plan for obtaining possession of the island and advised the minister at Madrid "to obtain correct information whether such a negotiation . . . is on foot . . . and, if so, to communicate to the Spanish government in a manner adapted to the delicacy of the case the sentiments of this government in relation to this subject, which are favorable to the continuance of Cuba in its connection with Spain. Clay made it more definite by telling Canning, "We would fight for Cuba should the British attempt the possession." This was before Monroe delivered his famous message.

Two years later, in 1825, the Monroe Doctrine first came

into play in connection with Cuba, although it was not specifically mentioned. Great Britain proposed a tripartite agreement with France and the United States, guaranteeing the neutralization of Cuba. The United States turned it down. Throughout the remainder of the first half of the century there were frequent diplomatic communications, addressed principally to Spain and England, reiterating the "hands off Cuba" policy of the United States, with increasingly stern language. In 1830 Secretary Van Buren said, "Possession should not be transferred from the Spanish Crown to any other power." In 1840 Secretary Forsyth told the minister at Madrid, "Should you have any reason to suspect any design on the part of Spain to transfer voluntarily her title to the island . . . you will distinctly state that the United States will prevent it at all hazard."

In 1843 Secretary Webster said, "The Spanish government has long been in possession of the policy and wishes of this government in regard to Cuba. . . . In the event of any attempt to wrest it from her, she might securely rely upon the whole naval and military resources of this country to aid her in preserving or recovering it." In 1848 Secretary Buchanan was moved by persistent rumors of Great Britain's desire to acquire Cuba to write, "We can never consent that this island shall become a colony of any other European power. In the possession of Great Britain or any strong naval power, it might prove ruinous both to our domestic and foreign commerce and even endanger the Union of the states. The highest and first duty of every independent nation is to provide for its own safety: and acting upon this principle we should be compelled to resist the acquisition of Cuba by any powerful maritime state with all the means which Providence has placed at our command."

In 1849 Secretary Clayton said it more simply. "The news of the cession of Cuba to any foreign power would, in the United States, be the instant signal for war." In those days it was recognized that foreign frigates in Havana harbor were as much a threat to the security of the United States as foreign missiles in the mountains of Cuba are today. Cuba has always been a spot where the basic reason for Monroe's message most strongly applied—a situation in which "our rights" might be "invaded or seriously menaced."

The first of the filibuster raids from the United States in the 1850s were directed against Cuba. They were led by Narciso López, a Venezuelan by birth who had become a general in the Spanish army in Cuba. He become a great advocate of Cuban freedom, and after his revolutionary plans were disclosed to the Spaniards, he fled to the United States. Here he found great popular support for his project to free Cuba and annex it to the United States, although the Government remained aloof from his plans. In fact, President Taylor squashed his first projected raid before it got started.

López insisted that the Cubans were ready to rise and throw off the yoke of Spain if they had leadership. He offered command of a second expedition to Jefferson Davis and then to Robert E. Lee. When these gentlemen turned him down he personally led six hundred men, mostly North Americans, on an invasion of Cuba. They landed successfully, raised the Cuban flag, and waited for the Cubans to rally to it. When nobody showed up but a handful of blacks, the Americans re-embarked and went home.

When he again invaded the island, in 1851, at the head of four hundred men, he was defeated, captured and publicly garroted. Fifty-two of his American followers were executed by firing squads.

England and France made a somewhat feeble effort to use the López raids as an excuse to intervene in Cuban affairs. They both dispatched naval vessels "to give assistance to Spain and to prevent by force the adventurers of any nation from landing with hostile intent on the island of Cuba." The United States replied with a statement that the López raiders had evaded the vigilance of the United States in embarking from New Orleans and that this "accident" could not be used to justify European intervention, because "the people of the United States were naturally jealous of European interference in American affairs."

In 1852, European fears that the United States would acquire Cuba again led to a proposal for a tripartite guarantee with France and England, which was to consist of a single clause reading, "The high contracting parties hereby severally and collectively disclaim now and for hereafter all intention to obtain possession of the Island of Cuba, and they respectively bind themselves to discountenance all attempt to that effect on the part of any power or individuals whatever."

Secretary of State Everett declined the proposed three-party convention in a long note which contained a thorough exposition of the United States policy relative to Cuba under the Monroe Doctrine. He said, "It is necessary only to cast one's eyes on the map to see how remote are the relations of Europe and how intimate those of the United States with this island." He contrasted the location of Cuba with an island in the Mediterranean, or at the mouth of the Seine or the Thames, and pointed out that, just as the European countries would not agree that the United States had an equal interest with them in any islands so located, "the condition of Cuba is mainly an American question." Although the United States had no plans for acquiring Cuba at the time, Everett said that this might not always be the case, because "under certain conditions it might be almost essential to our safety."

Although the note reiterated that the United States had no designs on Cuba, it was obvious that Everett was laying the groundwork for the acceptance of some change in its status. In connection with the ownership of Spain he said, "But can it be expected to last very long? Is it desirable that it should do so? Can it be for the interest of Spain to cling to a possession that can only be maintained by a garrison of twenty-five or thirty thousand troops? . . . Far from being really injured by the loss of this island, there is no doubt that, were it peacefully transferred to the United States, a prosperous commerce between Cuba and Spain, resulting from ancient associations and common language and tastes, would be far more productive than the best contrived system of colonial taxation." In short, everybody would be better off if Cuba belonged to the United States, but in any event, the political situation of Cuba was not the concern of any European country.

Although no administration in Washington would support the idea of acquiring Cuba through what was called the "Texas plan"—support to filibusters which would lead to first independence and then annexation—there was a keen desire in the Southern states to add this slave territory to the Union. President Polk tried to buy it in 1848, but the United States minister to Spain was told that "sooner than see the island transferred to any other power, they [the people of Spain] would prefer to see it sink in the ocean."

In 1854 the ire of Europe and Latin America was aroused by what looked like a definite plan on the part of the United States to conquer the island. James Buchanan, then ambassador to England, was vacationing in Ostend, Belgium, with the United States ambassadors to Spain and France. During the vacation Buchanan wrote, and the others signed, a long document addressed to the Secretary of State, which became known as the Ostend Manifesto. In it they proposed that the United States purchase Cuba for a sum not exceeding $120,000,000, pointing out that the "immediate acquisition" of the island was of "paramount importance" and any delay in getting it would be "exceedingly dangerous to the United States."

The document went on to say that "self-preservation is the first law of nature, with states as with individuals. . . . After we have offered Spain a price for Cuba far beyond its present value, and this shall have been refused . . . then, by every law, human and divine, we shall be justified in wresting it from Spain if we possess the power."

The Ostend Manifesto, coming as it did hard on the heels of the Mexican War, the acquisition of California and New Mexico, and filibuster raids from the United States was accepted throughout the world as final proof of Yankee imperialism—of the concept of the Monroe Doctrine that America was to be for the North Americans. Actually, the Manifesto had no support from the administration. Its prime purpose was to secure for Buchanan the support of the Southern states in obtaining the Democratic nomination for the presidency in 1856. In his acceptance speech he said that if he could first settle the slavery question "and then add Cuba to the Union" he would be "willing to give up the ghost." He did neither. Although a bill was introduced in the Senate in 1859 to appropriate $30,-000,000 as a down payment on Cuba, it died without coming to a vote.

After the 1860s there was a great change in the United States attitude toward Cuba and toward the European powers in relations involving Cuba. During the "golden age" of the Doctrine, when the United States was brandishing it at the slightest rumor of European action in the Western Hemisphere, there was no occasion to apply it to Cuba. France and England had given up any designs they may have had on the island—perhaps because they were convinced that any move in such direction would bring instant reaction from the United States. Annexation of Cuba by the United States was seldom mentioned for thirty years after the Civil War. When it was clear that nobody else would try to get it, the United States saw less need for possessing it. And the continued existence of Slavery in the island—which did not completely end until 1886—created a problem. All but the most ardent abolitionists were satiated with fighting about slavery.

During the ten years after 1868 when a revolution raged in Cuba, the United States showed a surprising lack of interest. The only relation of the Doctrine to this conflict was Grant's first enunciation of the "no transfer" principle, based on the possibility that the revolution might become the occasion for the transfer of sovereignty in the island from Spain to some other power.

When the United States finally intervened in the Cuban revolution to free the island from Spain in 1898, President

The Bettmann Archive

James Monroe delivered the message that became the Monroe
Doctrine

John Quincy Adams helped to conceive the Monroe Doctrine

James Polk reiterated the Monroe Doctrine

Henry E. Huntington Library and Art Gallery

Abraham Lincoln, in whose administration the Monroe Doctrine was first strongly challenged

Grover Cleveland, who used the Monroe Doctrine to challenge England

The Bettmann Archive

Theodore Roosevelt, who extended the meaning of the Monroe Doctrine

Franklin D. Roosevelt Library

Franklin Roosevelt, who shared the Monroe Doctrine with his
good neighbors

Courtesy of the White House

John Kennedy, who challenged Russia on the basis of the
Monroe Doctrine

McKinley made no effort to justify his request for intervention on the basis of the Doctrine, and there was surprisingly little reference to it in Congressional debate. The
Senate Committee on Foreign Relations, in reporting the
measure to the floor, did briefly refer to Monroe's dogma
by saying, "There are, it is stated, two policies, one of Europe, the other of the United States, each of which is based
distinctly upon the assertion of an intention to intervene
under certain circumstances. We refer to the principles of
the balance of power and the Monroe Doctrine. Each is a
distinct and arbitrary policy of intervention, to be effected
in certain contingencies in furtherance of national policies,
and to justify which no canon of international law was
ever invoked. . . . The latter [the Monroe Doctrine] . . .
was a distinct announcement that the United States would
intervene, under certain expressed circumstances, in the
affairs of every Central American and South American
state."

James Monroe would certainly have been surprised to
know that he had made a "distinct announcement" that
the United States had a right to intervene in the affairs of
every Latin American state. But the statement in the Committees' report passed without comment from either side
in the discussions preceding the war with Spain.

In Europe there was a great deal said about the Doctrine
at the time—all of it to the effect that the war with Spain
completely repudiated it. Monroe's words, "with the existing colonies or dependencies of any European power we
have not interfered and shall not interfere," were widely
quoted. In the minds of cynical Europeans the Doctrine
was being ignored when it interfered with the ruthless
march of Yankee imperialism.

Actually, at that time, there was nothing in the Cuban situation which warranted intervention in terms of national security. To the United States, the revolution at its doorstep was a nuisance and was interfering with commercial interests, but its result would be either the continuation of a weak Spanish colony or a weak independent state, neither of which involved the invocation of the Monroe Doctrine. President McKinley proposed intervention "in the name of humanity, in the name of civilization, in behalf of endangered American interests which give us the right and the duty to speak and to act."

McKinley was prodded into action by public opinion. It has often been said that the war with Spain was brought on by the American newspapers, partciularly those of William Randolph Hearst. Spanish atrocity stories, true or false, were fine circulation builders. They so aroused public sympathy for the oppressed Cubans that the sinking of the *Maine* in Havana harbor, from causes that have never been ascertained, brought on a popular demand for war.

The acquisition of Cuba by the United States as a result of the war was probably prevented by a young American attorney named Horatio Rubens. The Congressional resolution that authorized the President to intervene in Cuba did not say anything about what was to happen to the island after the fighting stopped. Rubens, a member of the Cuban Junta in the United States, rushed to Senator Teller of Colorado and said, "I tell you, Senator, the administration intends to steal the Island of Cuba. If you intend to give Cubans liberty why can you not say so?"

Teller quickly drafted an amendment which read, "That the United States hereby disclaims any disposition to exercise sovereignty, jurisdiction or control over said island except for the pacification thereof and asserts its determination when that is accomplished to leave the government and control of the island to its people." In the excitement the amendment was adopted without a vote. It undoubtedly prevented Cuba from becoming, like Puerto Rico, a dependency of the United States.

The Monroe Doctrine became more involved at the end of the war, and in connection with the Philippines and the almost coincidental annexation of Hawaii rather than with Cuba. The acquisition of both Pacific possessions was strongly attacked in Europe and by anti-expansionists at home on the basis that this was a violation of Monroe's thesis. It was maintained that the United States could not extend into the Eastern Hemisphere and at the same time deny other powers the right to possessions in the Western Hemisphere. In Congressional debate the "glaring inconsistency" of this policy was pointed out, and it was referred to as a rift in "our hitherto gnarled and unwedgeable oak," the Monroe Doctrine. Conservative newspapers referred to "the smashing of the Monroe Doctrine" and said that the Pacific expansion would "rend the Monroe Doctrine from top to bottom" and that the people of the United States would "think long before they exchange the right to guard the Western Hemisphere for the right of partnership in the colonizing schemes of European monarchies."

The attempts to use the Doctrine to oppose intervention in Cuba and expansion in the Pacific were not well founded. In the former case it was based on an unduly strict and unjustified interpretation of Monroe's phraseology. Monroe said that the United States "shall not interfere" with existing colonies—in 1823. He did not say "shall never interfere." There is absolutely no justification for assuming that the Doctrine meant that the *status quo* of 1823 should remain forever, no matter how the situation changed. At the time of Monroe's pronouncement the existing colonies represented no threat to the security of the United States, but if at any future time they did represent such a threat, the Doctrine could be invoked for such action as was necessary to assure national security. True, the Cuban situation was not a danger, but this did not deny the right of intervention under the Doctrine when danger existed.

As to the Pacific expansion, the Doctrine had nothing to do with it, one way or the other. At the time that Monroe delivered his message the United States had no Pacific coast. If, at some future time, Pacific possessions became desirable, there was nothing in the Doctrine that denied them. The Doctrine covered the special interest of the United States in the Western Hemisphere. It did not limit the interests of the United States to the Western Hemisphere.

By the end of the war with Spain public sentiment in the United States on behalf of the poor Cubans had died down. It was obvious that, in setting up a government in the island, some attention had to be paid to future relations with the United States. A Cuban committee drew up a constitution which made no reference to this important matter. It merely said that the "sentiment of gratitude toward the people of the United States" gave assurance that the two countries would "eternally maintain ties of the most intimate and eternal friendship."

In Washington this was not enough. American troops were still in Cuba, which was being administered by General Leonard Wood. In 1901 the Platt Amendment was tacked on to the Army Appropriations Act, and provided that American troops would stay in Cuba until the Cubans agreed to certain conditions. These included the right of the United States to intervene for the preservation of Cuban liberty and the protection of life and property; the right of the United States to supervise the public debt; the promise to continue the public health measures which the United States had started; and the granting of naval bases to the United States at certain specified points in Cuba.

The first article of the Platt Amendment was so pertinent in relation to later events that it should be quoted in full. It provided: "That the government of Cuba shall never enter into any treaty or other compact with any foreign power or powers which shall impair or tend to impair the independence of Cuba, nor in any manner authorize or permit any foreign power or powers to obtain by colonization or for military or naval purposes or otherwise, lodgement in or control over any portion of said island."

The Cubans did not like the Platt Amendment. They reluctantly accepted it, first as an amendment to their own constitution and then as a perpetual treaty with the United States. The treaty was abrogated in 1934.

Except for the two years that its affairs were administered by General Wood, Cuba has never had an honest, stable government. Wood supervised the first election, in which a capable president came into office. But the Cuban Congress could not understand this new system of free elections. They promptly changed the constitution to go back to the Spanish method of appointing, rather than electing, local officials. The party in power appointed the local officials. The election of the national government was supervised by police controlled by the local officials. Consequently, the party in power would stay in power until the next revolution. Few, if any, elections in Cuba have been honest, except when the United States again intervened for two years, starting in 1906.

From the end of the Spanish-American War until 1961 there was no occasion to apply the Monroe Doctrine to Cuba because it was, in reality, a protectorate of the United States—an economic protectorate. If Americans did not own the land on which the sugar was grown, American banks held the mortgages, American railroads transported the cane, American refineries crushed it and the United States bought it.

Regardless of whether or not this was good for the Cubans, it had a most unfortunate effect on political affairs. Graft was the accepted system of doing business with the Government. In Washington, the main interest was in a Cuban government under which commercial operations could be continued peacefully and profitably. On one occasion, in 1933, the United States sent Sumner Welles as a special ambassador to supervise the deposition of Cuba's first tyrant, Machado. This was the closest thing to outright political intervention in recent years.

The attitude of the United States toward Cuba during the reign of Fulgencio Batista, the dictator who preceded Fidel Castro, was well, if facetiously, expressed in an article by the humorist J. P. McEvoy in the *Saturday Evening Post* in 1939:

Cuba is not all rum and rumba. All the worries of the world can be found here in miniature. The soaring budget, the shrinking national income, the farm surplus, the rising cost of a policed peace, the class-conscious conflict, the indecisive democracy giving way to armed authority.

Theoretically she is an independent country, entitled to enjoy all her own headaches and hang-overs. Practically, she lives next door—only ninety miles away from her Uncle Sam, a crotchety old gentleman who doesn't hesitate to send a policeman when the party next door gets too noisy.

In a way, this confuses the gal. In one breath she is told to live her own life, but no sooner does she try to do this in her high spirited, if inexperienced, way, when Uncle Whiskers is back on the job, threatening to cut off her allowance.

"Do as you like!" says he, "but as long as you're depending on me for sugar, watch your step."

"Very well," says she defiantly, "I'll find myself another sugar daddy."

"Just try it," says Uncle Sam, pulling two guns out of his jeans and laying them on the mantel.

"Can't a girl live her own life?" and her dark Latin eyes fill with tears of rage.

"Sure," says Uncle Sam, stretching out on the sofa and putting his boots on the coffee table. "Sure, sure go as far as you like, little girl. Live your own life; your Uncle understands. That's what he's always done."

A knock at the door.

"*Guten Abend, senorita.*"

Uncle Sam sits up. "Tell that bum to get out of here."

The door closes and the dark-eyed miss storms into the room. Uncle Sam is lying quietly with a newspaper over his face. . . . He stirs himself.

"I think I'll go home now," he says. "See that your lights are out at nine o'clock. In case you need anything, don't bother me; remember, you're on your own." He pauses at the door. "Nice place you have here. Not a care in the world. You ought to be as happy as a bug in a rug."

Uncle Sam had no need for a Monroe Doctrine in dealing with his little niece—then. But the day would come.

In 1933 a Communist headquarters for Latin America was opened in Havana. Here was the best place to undermine United States influence and discredit Uncle Sam in the Western Hemisphere.

7

The Doctrine and the Ditch

On his last voyage to what he still thought was the edge of Asia, in 1502, Christopher Columbus sailed slowly along the coast of the Central American isthmus seeking the "secret of the strait" that would lead him to the wealth of the Orient. He glimpsed the western part of Panama before he turned away.

Eleven years later Vasco Nuñez de Balboa, governor of the province of Castilla del Oro (Darien), learned from the Indians that there was a great sea beyond the mountains that backed the Atlantic shore. He climbed the mountains. On September 25, 1513, he stood on top and gazed down at the waters of the Pacific. He looked back at the waters of the Atlantic. He said to himself, "There ought to be a road through here." Six years later the road was built—a paved road wide enough for two pack mules to pass each other. Before it was finished, Balboa had the Indians carry four disassembled brigantines across the mountains from the Atlantic to the Pacific—the first ships to cross the isthmus.

The road was suitable to bring gold and silver from Peru to Spanish galleons in the Atlantic. But a waterway would be much better to transport wool and indigo, dyewoods and mahogany from the Pacific possessions. Charles V of Spain instructed all his governors to explore bays and rivers in search of "the passage which would connect the eastern and western shores of the New World and shorten by two-thirds the route from Cadiz to Cathay."

Up in Mexico, Hernando Cortez obtained a map from Montezuma which led him to explore the Tehuantepec Peninsula. He found that the local Indians had a route across the isthmus, utilizing three rivers, which long antedated Balboa's in Panama, but it was not a connected waterway. González Dávila sailed north from Panama, landed on the Pacific coast of Nicaragua and climbed over the mountains to discover Lake Nicaragua. When it was later learned that this inland sea was connected with the Atlantic by the San Juan River, there was much excitement—which died down when it was discovered that there was no waterway for the short distance to the Pacific.

When it became apparent that there was no strait through the isthmus, thought turned to building one. In 1529 Cortez wrote to Charles V, "We have not found as yet a passage from Iberia to Cathay, but we must cut it. At no matter what cost, we must build a canal at Panama." The idea for the Panama Canal was not original with French Engineer Ferdinand de Lesseps or American President Theodore Roosevelt. Hernando Cortez had it almost four hundred years before the "big ditch" was dug.

For over three hundred years not much was done about it. When Philip II mounted the Spanish throne he put a stop to thoughts of canal building, believing that it would be counter to Divine Will to unite the oceans. Throughout the seventeenth and eighteenth centuries there were sporadic attempts at exploration. In 1698 a British colony was established at Darien by Scottish financier Paterson, founder of the Bank of England, which was designed to safeguard an isthmian route for the British at that point. The colony died out. In 1735 a French astronomer accompanied a Spanish scientific expedition in Nicaragua and later reported to the French Academy of Sciences that a canal was practical at that point—but nothing was done.

The first American interest in a canal is connected, as might be expected, with Benjamin Franklin, who was interested in everything. While he was minister to France in 1779 he received an unusual document signed "Pierre-André Garvaz, forçat numero 1336" (convict number 1336). The title of galley slave Garvaz's thesis was "Projet de paix Perpétuelle." One paragraph in it so aroused Franklin's interest that he printed the "Projet" on his press at Passy. It read:

There is the isthmus of Panama in America and that of Suez between Asia and Africa; these two isthmuses prevent the junction of four seas and are the reason that, to go around the world by water requires about three years and exposes one to stormy and very often icy seas and uninhabited coasts. Each of these two isthmuses must be cut from one sea to the other by a canal about sixty feet wide, thirty feet deep and about forty leagues long; by means of these two canals one will make the tour of the terrestrial globe, by water, in about ten months, and upon seas which are always good for navigation.

When Jefferson relieved Franklin in France he received a copy of Garvaz's "Projet" and indicated his interest in the canal question by writing to the chargé d'affaires in Madrid: "I have been told that the cutting of a canal through the isthmus of Panama, which the world has so often wished, and supposed practicable, has at times been thought of by the government of Spain. . . . I should be exceedingly pleased to get as minute details as possible on it and even copies of the surveys, reports, etc. if they could be obtained at a moderate expense."

Early in the nineteenth century world-wide interest in a Central American canal flared up when the German geographer von Humboldt spent five years exploring all possible routes. His writings led to a rash of canal projects in several countries. Spain set one up in 1814, but lost control of the area before it could function. The Congress of the Central American Republics passed a resolution in 1825 calling for a canal through Nicaragua. They gave a concession to an American group which included DeWitt Clinton, builder of the Erie Canal, but the North Americans were unable to raise the money. A Dutch group gained a concession in 1830 and tried to organize the Nicaraguan Canal Company, but a revolution back home put an end to this. A French company obtained a concession for a canal at Panama in 1838, and Louis Napoleon got a concession for the "Canale Napoléone de Nicaragua" in 1846. In addition, there were numerous surveys and reports by engineers of many nations.

During all this, none of these foreigners paid attention to the strangely prophetic words penned by, of all people, the German poet Goethe, who wrote in 1827: "I should wonder if the United States were to let an opportunity escape of getting such a work into their own hands. It may be foreseen that this young state, with its decided predilection to the west, will, in thirty or forty years, have occupied and peopled the large tract of land beyond the Rocky Mountains. . . . In such a case it would not only be desirable but almost necessary that a more rapid communication should be maintained between the eastern and western shores of North America. . . . I therefore repeat that it is absolutely indispensable for the United States to effect a passage from the Mexican Gulf to the Pacific Ocean; and I am certain that they will do it."

For many years the United States, too, ignored Goethe's prophecy. In 1826 the delegates to the first Inter-American Conference of Nations had been instructed that "A cut or a canal for the purposes of navigation somewhere through the isthmus that connects the two Americas, to unite the Pacific and Atlantic Oceans, will form a proper subject of consideration at the Congress." But the United States delegates arrived too late to consider anything. During the Jackson and Van Buren administrations some rather half-hearted attempts were made to negotiate with the Central American states in relation to a canal. In 1849 a New York group secured a franchise to build a railroad across Panama. They built it and talked about a canal. Cornelius Vanderbilt's combination boat and stagecoach line across Nicaragua, which contributed to the filibuster Walker's downfall, also contained a provision for a canal. But none of these things went beyond the survey stage.

The first diplomatic negotiation by the United States involving a canal was a treaty with New Granada (later Colombia, which included Panama) in 1846. This treaty provided: "The government of New Granada guarantees to the government of the United States that the right of way of transit across the Isthmus of Panama upon any modes of communication that now exist, or that may be hereafter constructed, shall be open and free to the government and citizens of the United States. . . . And, in order to secure to themselves the tranquil and constant enjoyment of these advantages, the United States guarantee . . . to New Granada, by the present stipulation, the perfect neutrality of the before-mentioned isthmus . . . and also guarantee, in the same manner, the rights of sovereignty and property which New Granada has and possesses over the said territory."

On the face of it, this treaty was a fine example of inter-American joint action in the best tradition of Mr. Monroe's message—except that, in transmitting it, the United States suggested to New Granada that they secure similar agreements from France and England. This would, in effect, make a tripartite agreement securing New Granada's rights involving two European powers—a direct contradiction of Monroe's principle.

During the late 1840s British aggression in Central America was at its peak, although the initiative was more on the part of local English officials than the home government. Frederick Chatfield, the British minister to the five Central American Republics, was the principal agent in using the Mosquito "nation" to exert fictional claims on extended territory. His aggression was met by local United States officials. Elijah Hise, chargé d'affaires at Guatemala, negotiated a treaty with Nicaragua covering the right of way for a canal, under which the United States guaranteed the integrity of Nicaragua. It was never ratified and Hise was replaced by Ephraim Squier. This agent negotiated another treaty and secured the contract for Vanderbilt's company to build a canal.

Squier went further. He induced Honduras to cede Tigre Island, on the Pacific side of the isthmus, to the United States for eighteen months, and to permit a naval base on the Gulf of Fonseca to guard the Pacific end of the canal. When Chatfield heard of this he ordered the captain of a British man-of-war to seize the island and raise the English flag. Squier said this was a violation of American territory and delivered an ultimatum, saying that if the English did not get out in six days it would be an act of aggression toward the United States. Fortunately, a level-headed British admiral, who knew the attitude of the home government better than the hotheaded local diplomats, lowered the flag and sailed away.

All of this pointed up the need for some kind of action between Washington and London—either a fight or a compromise. It was somewhat similar to the situation in Cuba. Neither nation, then, wanted to have exclusive control over a canal through the isthmus—but neither wanted the other to have it. Secretary of State Clayton wrote: "We are deeply anxious to avoid any collision with the British government in relation to this matter; but that collision will become inevitable if great prudence is not exercised on both sides. . . . When Great Britain shall ascertain the real objects that we have in view she cannot, I think, fail to see the propriety of aiding instead of obstructing us in securing for all nations, on the same terms, the right of passage by the Nicaragua route from ocean to ocean."

These negotiations led to the Clayton-Bulwer treaty between the United States and Great Britain in 1850. This treaty provided that neither government would "ever

maintain for itself any exclusive control" over the Nicaraguan canal, and that neither would "ever erect or maintain
any fortifications commanding the same, or in the vicinity
thereof, or occupy, or fortify, or colonize or assume, or
exercise any dominion over Nicaragua, Costa Rica, the
Mosquito Coast, or any part of Central America."

Whig Clayton was no Monroeist. He had sneered at
Polk's reiteration of the Doctrine a few years before, and
during the negotiations on the treaty, he told the British
minister that President Zachary Taylor did not agree with
his predecessor on the dogma. The treaty was obviously a
refutation of the principle enunciated by Monroe, in that
it sanctified British participation in the political situation
of part of the Western Hemisphere. But, in 1850, nobody
mentioned this. It was good to have some seeming settlement of the Central American disturbances, even if the
settlement violated the principle of the Doctrine. And,
Monroe's message had not yet become gospel—it had not
even gained the sacred name of Doctrine.

After the treaty was signed Vanderbilt's company started
to survey the Nicaragua route. Then it was realized that
Great Britain should participate. British engineers studied
the survey. Before they finished, William Walker had em-
barked upon his conquest of Nicaragua. When the Nicara-
guans regained control of their country, feeling against the
United States ran so high that the concession to Vanderbilt's Accessory Transit Company was revoked.

There were various canal projects during the remainder
of the 1850s and the 1860s involving the United States,
England and France in Colombia, Honduras and Nicaragua; but nothing materialized. Then in 1869 occurred two
events on opposite sides of the world that deflected atten-

tion from an isthmian canal for a time. A gold spike was driven fifty-three miles west of Ogden, Utah to complete the first transcontinental railroad. The Atlantic and Pacific coasts were brought closer together without a canal.

In that same year the French engineer Ferdinand de Lesseps finished cutting through the other isthmus mentioned by convict Garvaz in the "Projet" he had sent to Benjamin Franklin, and the first ship sailed from the Mediterranean to the Red Sea through the Suez Canal. With the opening of this short cut to India, British interest in canals shifted from Central America to the Mediterranean.

Nine years passed. In 1878 the canal policy of the United States radically changed, and the Monroe Doctrine came dramatically to the fore. The occasion was the formation, in Paris, of *La Compagnie Universelle du Canal Interocéanique de Panama*. This French company had secured a concession from Colombia, and the great De Lesseps was to build a canal.

By this time the Doctrine was in full flower, and the idea of a French-owned canal in the Western Hemisphere was, in the opinion of the press, the people and the Congress, a horrible violation of it. The House Committee on Interocean Canals reported out a resolution to the effect that any form of protectorate or other attempt by any European government to control an independent state on this continent is contrary to the Monroe Doctrine and dangerous to the peace, prosperity and safety of the United States; that the United States asserts and maintains its right to possess and control any artificial means of communication across the isthmus; and that the President is requested to take steps for the abrogation of any treaty in conflict with this declaration.

In connection with the canal, President Hayes told Congress: "The United States cannot consent to the surrender of this control to any European power or any combination of European powers. . . . The capital invested by corporations or citizens of other countries in such an enterprise must in a great degree look for protection to one or more of the great powers of the world. No European power can intervene for such protection without adopting measures on this continent which the United States would deem wholly inadmissable." He continued to say that a canal would be, "the great ocean thoroughfare between our Atlantic and Pacific shores and virtually part of the coastline of the United States."

At no other time has so much been written and said about the principle underlying Monroe's message. General Grant spoke from retirement, saying, "In accordance with the early and later policy of the government, in obedience to the often expressed will of the American people, with a due regard to our national dignity and power, with a watchful care for our interests and industries on this continent, and with the determination to guard against even the first approach of rival powers, whether friendly or hostile, on these shores, I commend an American canal, on American soil, to the American people."

A prominent congressman soberly summarized popular opinion with this statement: "In every conflict of European with American interest on the two Western continents our countrymen make their appeal to the Monroe Doctrine. It is quoted as the supreme, indisputable and irreversible judgment of our national union. Of the very few maxims which serve to guide public opinion in our country, this ranks as the chief. . . . It has also taken fast hold on the popular mind. A President of the United States, justly appealing to it in an emergency, could not fail of unanimous following of patriotic citizens, even in the presence of a consequently impending war."

Actually, the Doctrine had no direct application to the French canal-building activity in Colombia. This was a private undertaking by a commercial company. The Quai d'Orsay had informed the United States, even before the storm rose, that the French government had no hand in the matter, would not interfere nor accept any responsibility. But the United States minister in Bogotá advised Washington that Colombia was negotiating with European states to guarantee the neutrality of the canal. Upon receipt of this information, Secretary of State Blaine sent a communication to all United States diplomats in Europe saying that this would never do. Such a foreign guarantee would be, he said, "of the nature of an alliance against the United States" in view of "the pronounced adherence of the United States to principles long since enunciated by the highest authority of the government, and now, in the judgment of the President, firmly confirmed as an integral part of our national policy."

Blaine's first note ignored the existence of the Clayton-Bulwer treaty, but with the state of mind that then existed this agreement was considered the most pernicious of entangling foreign alliances in violation of the Monroe Doctrine. Blaine sent another note to England requesting the modification or cancellation of the treaty on the grounds that the United States could not prolong "any treaty that impeaches our rightful and long established claim to priority on the American continent." He reiterated the point that President Hayes had made relative to the canal being virtually part of the coast line of the United States. British Foreign Secretary Lord Granville answered politely, agreeing to nothing, and rather sarcastically inquiring whether, under this extension of the coast line, the states between the canal and the United States would retain their independence.

Blaine's successor, Secretary Frelinghuysen, next took up the crusade with a long note outlining the history of canal negotiations and of the Monroe Doctrine. This elicited a more pointed reply from Lord Granville in which he said, "The views which were entertained by President Monroe have not always been accepted by his successors; nor have the same views always been entertained either by the American Congress or by the Secretaries of State of the United States; but the mere fact that a treaty was concluded between this country and the United States in 1850 (twenty-seven years after the so-called 'Monroe Doctrine' was enunciated), for the express purpose of establishing communication by ship-canal across the isthmus of Central America, and of jointly protecting any such communications which might be made, is a clear proof that neither the American administration of that day nor the United States Congress that sanctioned the treaty considered that they were precluded by the utterances of President Monroe in 1823 from entering into such a treaty with one or more of the European powers. How, then, can it be said, at the present day, that the Clayton-Bulwer treaty is opposed to the Monroe Doctrine?"

Lord Granville obviously had a point. He could not be answered by the true explanation—that the public attitude toward the Monroe Doctrine in 1882 was vastly different from the attitude that had prevailed in 1850. No further requests were made for the abrogation of the treaty in terms of the Doctrine. Instead a treaty was made with Nicaragua covering an American owned and operated canal. The Senate would not sanction this outright violation of the Clayton-Bulwer treaty and refused to ratify the Nicaraguan treaty.

And so the matter stood for eighteen years. During this period De Lesseps' French company went into bankruptcy, was reorganized and again failed. The French canal was no longer an active threat. The Monroe Doctrine may have played a part in the failure of De Lesseps' company. The French Government considered guaranteeing its bonds, so as to give it another chance, but refrained from doing so in deference to the position taken by the United States. The Frenchmen next turned to Great Britain, saying: "Why not make France's loss Britain's gain, take over the uncompleted works and give the world an all-British canal across the Isthmus of Panama?" The Monroe Doctrine stood squarely in the way of even considering such a proposal.

Meanwhile, England had, through negotiations fostered by the United States, corrected most of the abuses which her former aggressive policy in Central America had brought about. She had given up her claims to sovereignty over Greytown, at the mouth of the San Juan River—an essential entry point for a Nicaraguan canal—and the ubiquitous Mosquitoes were on a reservation removed from the canal route. There was nothing left of the objectionable Clayton-Bulwer treaty except the bipartite supervision of a canal and the prohibition against fortifications.

The Spanish-American War brought a new flare-up of interest in the United States for a canal across the isthmus. During the war the dramatic and dangerous dash of the battleship *Oregon* from the Pacific around the Horn had pointed up the military advantages. The acquisition of the Philippines and the annexation of Hawaii created obvious added commercial advantages. Renewed efforts were made to change the Clayton-Bulwer treaty. They first resulted in an agreement that modified, but did not abrogate, the older treaty. Specifically, the United States might build a canal independently, but could not fortify it. Also, the canal was to be completely neutralized, open even to enemy warships.

This proposed treaty brought the first comment on the subject from a man who was to have much to do with the canal—and with the Monroe Doctrine. From Albany, New York's Governor, Theodore Roosevelt, wrote condemning, first, the military aspect of the agreement, pointing out that, although the *Oregon* could have come through the canal from the Pacific, the Spanish fleet of Admiral Cervera could likewise have gone through to the Pacific to fight Dewey at Manila or attack the defenseless Pacific Coast— if the canal were completely neutral. He then added:

"Secondly, as to the Monroe Doctrine. If we invite foreign powers to a joint ownership, a joint guarantee, of what so vitally concerns us but a little way from our borders, how can we possibly object to similar joint action say in Southern Brazil or Argentina, where our interests are so much less evident? If Germany has the same right that we have in the canal across Central America, why not in the partition of any part of Southern America? To my mind we should consistently refuse to all European powers the right to control, in any shape, any territory in the Western Hemisphere which they do not already hold." Roosevelt's specific reference to Germany in connection with the canal is confusing except in light of the fact that he already sensed that Germany was the ultimate enemy.

Finally, in 1902, England agreed to the complete abrogation of the Clayton-Bulwer treaty, opening the way for an all-American canal without any conditions. It cannot be said that the Monroe Doctrine directly was responsible for this, but it played a part in the background. Because of the current world attitude toward her position in the Boer War, Great Britain wanted the good will of the United States. That good will was not possible while she held to a treaty which the American people insisted was a violation of their precious Doctrine.

The Monroe Doctrine had nothing to do with the rest of the story of "the big ditch." But the rest of the story had much to do with the Monroe Doctrine, in that it was a great step backward in inter-American affairs. Also, the canal contributed to a change in United States policy in the Caribbean area, and the Monroe Doctrine was reinterpreted to justify that change.

After the abrogation of the Clayton-Bulwer treaty it was assumed that the canal would be built through Nicaragua. But a young Frenchman named Philippe Bunau-Varilla had other ideas. He had been an engineer for the French company and was dedicated to a canal through Panama. He lobbied in Washington with such great zeal that a commission was appointed to estimate the costs of canals by both routes. They reported that a canal at Nicaragua would cost $189,864,062 while one at Panama would cost $144,233,358—plus $109,141,500 that the French company was asking for its holdings. They recommended a canal through Nicaragua, and a bill for its construction passed the House. When the French company heard this they lowered their asking price for their Panama holdings to $40,000,000.

Meanwhile, Bunau-Varilla had reached President Theodore Roosevelt and convinced him of the superiority of the Panama route. Before the canal bill came up in the Senate, nature gave the zealous Frenchman an unusual assist. Volcanic Mt. Pelée on the island of Martinique erupted and made banner headlines by wiping out the city of St. Pierre, the greatest volcanic disaster since Pompeii.

Bunau-Varilla promptly bought ninety Nicaraguan stamps which pictured volcanic Mt. Momotombo in Nicaragua. He sent one to each Senator with a note that said, in effect, "Volcanoes are so symbolic of Nicaragua that they put them on their postage stamps. The last time this one erupted it dumped a train, a wharf and a coffee warehouse into a lake that would be part of a Nicaraguan canal."

Although Senator Morgan, proponent of the Nicaraguan canal route, started his speech supporting the House bill by saying: "I do not care to approach the discussion of this important measure in a cloud of volcanic smoke and ashes which the opponents of the measure outside the Senate have brought as a funeral pall to place over its bier," the horrible thought of molten lava steaming into the canal was too much for his colleagues. They amended the bill to authorize the President to acquire the French holdings in Panama and to acquire from Colombia control of a canal zone. If either of these acquisitions was not possible the President was directed to proceed with the construction of the Nicaraguan canal.

A treaty was promptly drawn under which Colombia was to receive $10,000,000 plus an annuity of $250,000 for a canal zone completely under United States control. The Colombians did not like it. They wanted more money. And, they pointed out, the cession of sovereignty over part of their territory to the United States was counter to the treaty of 1846 with New Granada, which was still in force, under which the United States guaranteed "the rights of sovereignty and property which New Granada has and possesses over said territory." The United States Navy had helped to suppress seven insurrections in Panama, six of them at Colombia's request, since the original treaty had been drawn.

Colombia hoped that she could get somebody else to finish the French canal on more favorable terms. While her Congress wrangled over ratification of the treaty, Bunau-Varilla cabled the Colombian President: "One must admit as a fundamental principle the only party that can now build the Panama Canal is the United States and that neither European governments nor private financiers would dare to fight either the Monroe Doctrine or the American Treasury for building the Panama Canal, in case Americans return to Nicaragua." The Colombian Congress turned down the treaty.

There had been a serious revolution in Panama against Colombian rule a few years before, which was suppressed with the help of United States Marines. There was still a revolutionary committee in Panama City. After again meeting with Roosevelt and Secretary of State Hay, Bunau-Varilla assured the committee that, if Panama again revolted, the United States would not permit Colombia to use force in suppressing the uprising. When the committee asked for more definite assurance, Bunau-Varilla cabled that there would be an American warship at Colón in forty-eight hours.

The revolution was set for November 3. The gunboat *Nashville* was ordered to Colón, on the Atlantic side of the isthmus, on October 30. The *Marblehead* and the *Boston* were ordered to Panama, on the Pacific side, on November 2, with orders to "prevent landing of any armed force, either government or insurgent, with hostile intent within fifty miles of Panama." Before the *Nashville* reached Colón four hundred Colombian troops had been landed. The *Nashville*'s commander held them there, permitting only two officers to proceed to Panama City, where they were arrested by the revolutionaries.

The revolutionary forces at Panama City consisted of 441 policemen and firemen and 500 Colombian troops who had been bribed to change sides, possibly with private money from the United States. On the evening of November 3, 1903, they raised the Panamanian flag and declared the independence of the Republic of Panama. The Colombian troops at Colón were induced to return to Cartagena by the payment of $8,000 and two cases of champagne for the colonel. The revolution was not entirely bloodless. One Colombian gunboat that had not been bought off hurled six shells into Panama City, killing a donkey in a slaughter-house and a Chinaman in his bed.

The Colombian government cabled Washington for permission to land troops at Colón and Panama City to quell the revolt. Secretary Hay replied that it was "not thought desirable to permit landing of Colombian troops on isthmus, as such a course would precipitate civil war and disturb for an indefinite period the free transit which we are pledged to protect." By some perverted logic, Hay was applying *against* Colombia the provisions of the treaty *with* Colombia.

Washington received official notification of Panamanian independence on November 5. One day, seventeen hours and forty-one minutes later Secretary Hay cabled recognition of the new government. Twelve days later Bunau-Varilla, as Minister Plenipotentiary of Panama, signed a treaty covering the cession of the Canal Zone to the United States—on the latter's terms.

This first use of "the big stick" in Latin America is difficult to justify in terms of international law, the treaty with Colombia or the Monroe Doctrine. There is no proof that Roosevelt instigated the revolution or that he promised Bunau-Varilla beforehand that the United States Navy would intervene to assure its success. But Roosevelt himself said, in relation to the latter point, that Bunau-Varilla would have been "a very dull man" had he been unable to make "a very accurate guess" as to "what our government would do."

Roosevelt later justified his actions by saying, "The people of Panama were a unit in desiring the canal and in wishing to overthrow the rule of Colombia. If they had not revolted, I should have recommended to Congress to take possession of the isthmus by force of arms. . . . When they revolted, I promptly used the Navy to prevent the bandits, who tried to hold us up, from spending months of futile bloodshed . . . to the lasting damage of the isthmus, of us, and of the world." On another occasion he said, simply, "I took the Canal Zone."

Up until that time the intervention of the United States in the internal affairs of the independent states of Latin

America was not contemplated by the Monroe Doctrine. Certainly, in spirit at least, the Doctrine was opposed to such action. And there is no question that the action of the United States was a violation of the 1846 treaty with Colombia and of the basic canons of international law. Of it the distinguished historian Samuel Bemis said:

With patience, diplomacy could have secured control of a canal route in a more creditable way without the use of force. The episode antagonized Latin America. Public opinion there began to brand the sponsor-nation of the Monroe Doctrine with the accusation of conquest in that part of the world which it professed to have liberated from European interference.

And after the canal episode the situation worsened. During the next quarter century the Doctrine would be reinterpreted to justify widespread intervention in the Caribbean area. At one time or another the United States either owned, partially controlled or established protectorates over all the Central American mainland except British Honduras and the Yucatan Peninsula and every important island except Jamaica.

8

Dollar Diplomacy and the Big Stick

Theodore Roosevelt was a man of action. Like most such men he combined great enthusiasm with small patience. To him, a straight line was the shortest distance between an objective and its accomplishment—and therefore the proper course. The circumlocutions of diplomacy were foreign to his nature. If a thing needed to be done, the way to get it done was to *do it*—not talk about it.

Theodore Roosevelt was an imperialist. He believed that backward peoples, or states which could not maintain a stable government, were better off under the control of more advanced societies. He said, "Every expansion of civilization makes for peace. In other words, every expansion of a great civilized power means a victory for law, order and righteousness."

But in practice, Roosevelt's imperialism was not primarily idealistic nor materialistic. It related to his zeal for national strength. He said, "No friendliness with other nations, no good will for them or by them, can take the place of national self-reliance." And again, "Diplomacy is utterly useless where there is not force behind it; the diplomat is the servant, not the master, of the soldier."

Theodore Roosevelt was thoroughly in accord with the Monroe Doctrine, but he believed that its strength lay in the ability of the United States to enforce it. "In public as in private life a bold front tends to insure peace and not strife." And, he said, "There is a homely adage which runs 'Speak softly and carry a big stick; you will go far.' If the American nation will speak softly and yet build and keep at a pitch of the highest training a thoroughly efficient navy, the Monroe Doctrine will go far."

Some of the Latin American states did not conform to Roosevelt's concept of civilization. In justifying his actions toward Colombia in the canal episode he later said, "To talk of Colombia as a responsible power to be dealt with as we would deal with Holland or Belgium or Switzerland or Denmark is a mere absurdity. The analogy is with a group of Sicilian or Calabrian bandits. . . . You could no more make an agreement with the Colombian rulers than you could nail currant jelly to a wall—and the failure to nail currant jelly to a wall is not due to the nail; it is due to the currant jelly."

When he assumed the Presidency after the assassination of McKinley in 1901 there were things which, in his opinion, had to be done in the interest of national security. One of them was the canal question, which he handled in a typically Rooseveltian manner. Others involved the security of the area which the United States must, in his opinion, dominate in order to assure the safety of the canal —things such as the naval base at Guantanamo which he established under the Platt Amendment.

Although he was more interested in accomplishment than in policy, he realized that "It would be well-nigh impossible, even if it were not highly undesirable, for this country to carry out any policy save one that had become part of the inherited tradition of the country, like the Monroe Doctrine." If the policy which he wanted to pursue needed the support of the Monroe Doctrine, the obvious thing to do was to change the Monroe Doctrine to support it. And so was born the "Roosevelt Corollary" to the Monroe Doctrine.

The Corollary was contained in Roosevelt's annual message to Congress in 1904. In part he said:

It is not true that the United States feels any land hunger or entertains any projects as regards the other nations of the Western Hemisphere save such as are for their welfare. All that this country desires is to see the neighboring countries stable, orderly and prosperous. Any country whose people conduct themselves well can count upon our hearty friendship. If a nation shows that it knows how to act with reasonable efficiency and decency in social and political matters, if it keeps order and pays its obligations, it need fear no interference from the United States. Chronic wrongdoing, or an impotence which results in a general loosening of the ties of civilized society, may in America as elsewhere, ultimately require intervention by some civilized nation, and in the Western Hemisphere the adherence of the United States to the Monroe Doctrine may force the United States, however reluctantly, in flagrant cases of such wrongdoing or impotence, to the exercise of an international police power. . . .

Our interests and those of our southern neighbors are in

reality identical. . . . If within their borders the reign of law and order obtains, prosperity is sure to come to them. While they thus obey the primary laws of civilized society they may rest assured that they will be treated by us in a spirit of cordial and helpful sympathy. We would interefere with them only in the last resort, and then only if it became evident that their inability or unwillingness to do justice at home and abroad had violated the rights of the United States or had invited foreign aggression to the entire body of American nations.

The specific excuse for the establishment of the Corollary had to do with the debts of Central American states to European nationals. It was common practice for presidents or dictators in many of the Caribbean states, upon coming into power, to float a loan with foreign bankers, securing it by promising that the customs duties collected at one or more ports of entry would be sequestered to pay the loan or the interest. In other cases concessions were sold to foreigners to construct and operate utilities or railroads, or to develop mineral rights. Frequently, much of the money so derived went into the pockets of the party in power. When the government changed, usually by revolution, the incoming administration would not or could not honor the obligations. The foreign financiers turned to their governments to protect their interests. The best way to do it was for the European powers to take over the collection of Latin American customs. This involved occupation of the territory of the defaulting country.

Shortly after Roosevelt took office such a situation threatened in Venezuela. A particularly obnoxious dictator named Cipriano Castro was seven years in arrears on the interest on bonds held by German bankers, had not paid dividends on the railroad which Germans had built in

Venezuela, and had not compensated German nationals for losses incurred during the revolution that brought him into power. Britain and Italy had similar claims as, to a lesser extent, did other European countries and the United States.

Germany frankly advised the United States that she proposed to take coercive action against Venezuela in conjunction with England and Italy. The action would include a blockade of the principal harbors and the seizure of Venezuelan gunboats. If this did not work, the Germans said that they would "have to consider the temporary occupation of . . . different Venezuelan harbor places and the levying of duties in those places." However, said the German note, "We declare especially that under no circumstances do we consider in our proceedings the acquisition or the permanent occupation of Venezuelan territory."

At first, this proposal was accepted calmly by the United States State Department. Secretary John Hay replied: "The Monroe Doctrine is a declaration that there must be no territorial aggrandizement by any non-American power at the expense of any American power on American soil. . . . This Doctrine has nothing to do with the commercial relations of any American power. . . . We do not guarantee any state against punishment if it misconducts itself, providing that the punishment does not take the form of the acquistion of territory by any non-American power."

Although the State Department was willing to accept Germany's assurance, the American people were not so acquiescent. Public opinion was decidedly suspicious of Germany. During the five years previous the "big navy" group in Germany had developed into a strong faction. They wanted bases in the Western Hemisphere. During the Spanish-American War Admiral von Tirpitz had openly advocated action to secure such a base while the United States was busy in Cuba. The purchase of the Danish West Indies was considered. Von Tirpitz also talked about Curaçao, a coaling station in Brazil, the Galápagos and Dutch Guiana.

When the United States queried the German Foreign Office on its intentions, with a reminder of the principles of the Doctrine, the Wilhelmstrasse piously denied any evil intent, saying, "All the reports that are circulated concerning German plans of conquest in South and Central America are lies and slanders of our enemies."

But in the United States people were not willing to believe this. They knew that Germany had little respect for the precious Doctrine. Old Bismarck had growled from retirement that the Monroe Doctrine was a "species of arrogance peculiarly American and inexcusable. . . . The Monroe Doctrine is a spectre that would vanish in plain daylight." The German Kaiser had claimed that the Doctrine had died with the Spanish-American War and that what was best for the German navy must be done, "even if it displeases the Yankees."

As soon as the Germans, British and Italians established their blockade, Venezulea appealed to the United States in terms of the Monroe Doctrine and requested that the matter be submitted to arbitration. When the United States passed this on to the foreign powers, Germany immediately agreed, followed by the others. Further, they suggested that Roosevelt act as arbitrator—a position which he reluctantly declined because the United States was one of the minor claimants. The matter was submitted to the Hague Tribunal.

There is some difference of opinion as to why Germany quickly about-faced and agreed to arbitrate, after so ostentatiously clenching the mailed fist. Fifteen years later, Roosevelt claimed that it was due to a direct action of his in forcefully brandishing the Monroe Doctrine. In 1916 he wrote a long letter in which he described in detail an ultimatum which he had verbally delivered to the German ambassador. Roosevelt claimed that he had told the Ambassador "to inform his government that if no notification for arbitration came within a certain specified number of days I should be obliged to order Dewey to take his fleet to the Venezuelan coast and see that the German forces did not take possession of any territory. . . . Less than twenty-four hours before the time I had appointed for cabling the order to Dewey, the embassy notified me that His Imperial Majesty the German Emperor had directed him to request me to undertake the arbitration myself."

Although this has found its way into some Roosevelt biographies, and into numerous histories, it is questionable whether the conversation ever took place as Roosevelt recalled it. If it did, there is no record that the German ambassador ever reported it to Berlin. Nor is there any documentary reference to it in United States archives. Roosevelt's appointment calendar showed no meeting with the German ambassador at or near the time when the conversation was supposed to have taken place. In fact there could not have been such a meeting—the German ambassador was not in Washington. Roosevelt repeated the sense of the ultimatum story in two speeches in 1917. It is probable that his imagination was better than his memory, and that he was inspired, in the letter and speeches, by the bitter feeling against Germany shortly prior to America's entry into World War I.

It is far more likely that, aside from what Roosevelt may have told the German ambassador, the Reich backed down as a result of the reports that they received on the strong feeling of the American people against foreign pressure on Venezuela. Regardless of whether the State Department felt that "the Doctrine has nothing to do with the commercial relations of any American power," the public felt, as they had in connection with the Venezulean boundary dispute a few years before, that Germany was violating the Doctrine. The German ambassador described the attitude of the American public as a "truly hysterical demonstration."

And there is no question that England's reaction was based on the outburst of feeling reported from the United States. The Prime Minister said, "We welcome any increase in the influence of the United States of America in the Western Hemisphere. We desire no colonization, we desire no alteration in the balance of power, we desire no acquisition of territory. We have not the slightest intention of interfering with the mode of government in any portion of that continent. The Monroe Doctrine is not really in question at all." The Foreign Secretary echoed the British position on the Doctrine: "Nothing should be done to give offense to the susceptibilities of the United States, or to indicate in any way that we have any desire to impugn the Monroe Doctrine." Another member of the Ministry said: "The principle of the Monroe Doctrine has always received the unwavering support of successive Ministries in this country, and no temporary inconvenience will cause us to waver in our adhesion to the policy of the American people."

There had been quite a change in the British attitude toward the Monroe Doctrine since Lord Salisbury had written, in connection with the boundary dispute, seven years before, that his note must not "be understood as acceptance of it on the part of Her Majesty's Government." It might be noted in passing that, in the interim, the United States fleet had been greatly expanded. Even Germany had a new respect for the Doctrine. When the German ambassador was replaced, as a result of the Venezulean affair, the new diplomat said, as soon as he got off the boat, "The Emperor understands the Monroe Doctrine thoroughly. . . . He appreciates the American feeling for the Monroe Doctrine, and would not think of occupying a coaling station or territory. He would no more think of violating that Docrtine, than he would of colonizing the moon."

This Venezulean dispute was partially responsible for the Roosevelt Corollary. When the Hague Tribunal arbitrated the matter it ruled that the claims of the nations which had taken action to collect the debts—Germany, England and Italy—should have priority. This obviously placed a premium on armed intervention for the collection of debts. Also, the type of negotiation that was involved in the Venezuelan matter was foreign to Roosevelt's nature. He wanted more direct and independent action. When a similar situation developed in Santo Domingo, he decided that the United States would play policeman, collect the customs duties and administer justice to the debtors.

The Corollary was based on the Archimedean-type premise that for every right there is an equal and opposite responsibility. If the United States claimed certain special rights in the Western Hemisphere, should it not also have certain special responsibilities? As with Monroe's initial message, this premise was originally advanced by England. As early as 1861, when the United States ambassador at Mexico City had denounced the right of foreign intervention that was ostensibly to compel payment of debts, the British minister had replied, "If the position of the United States . . . is maintained, I cannot but view it as binding that country to assume the moral obligation toward other nations of restoring peace and order in Mexico, and of preventing scenes which disgrace humanity and neutralize . . . the international rights and commercial relations of civilized nations."

In 1895 Lord Salisbury used the question of the responsibility—or lack of responsibility—of the United States for the actions of Latin American states as a telling argument in his refutation of the application of the Monroe Doctrine to the Venezuelan border dispute. He said, "Whatever may be the authority of the doctrine laid down by President Monroe, there is nothing in his language to show that he ever thought of claiming this novel prerogative for the United States. It is admitted that he did not seek to assert a protectorate over Mexico or the states of Central and South America. Such a claim would have imposed upon the United States the duty for answering for the conduct of these states, and consequently the responsibility of controlling it. . . . It follows of necessity that if the government of the United States will not control the conduct of these communities, neither can it protect them for the consequences attached to any misconduct of which they may be guilty towards other nations."

In 1903 the London *Times* expressed it more directly by saying: "The power which holds the shield over the weaker states is under an obligation to compel them to observe their duties in regard to others."

Also, the idea of the United States taking over supervision of Latin American customs collections was not new. It had been proposed in connection with Venezuela in 1869 and again in 1881. But, since it involved either intervention in the affairs of a Latin American state or a form of protectorate, Congress would never approve of it until Roosevelt related it to an established policy—the sacred Doctrine.

The situation in Santo Domingo to which the Corollary was first applied had been brewing long before Roosevelt came into office. One of the most vicious dictators in history, Ulises Heureaux, came into power in 1886. When he was assassinated in 1899 he left a record of over two thousand murders and a public debt of $20,000,000. There followed a series of revolutions until, in 1904, an ex-priest named Carlos Morales was chosen president as a compromise candidate by two revolutionary groups. It is possible that the United States had something to do with this. At least, the compromise was made on the deck of the cruiser *Detroit*.

For years prior to this, bankers of several foreign countries had been trying unsuccessfully to collect from Santo Domingo. There is some question as to how much sympathy they deserve. There is a record of one loan of £757,-700 on which the Dominicans agreed to pay principal and interest of £58,900 annually for twenty-five years, guaranteed by the customs revenues of two ports, the royalties from guano sales and the revenue from mines and forests of one province. However, the Dominicans claimed that they received only £38,000 out of the whole transaction.

During 1903 and 1904 several European creditors were threatening intervention to collect. And there were other side lights. There were persistent rumors that one of the "out" parties in Santo Domingo was trying to gain the support of Germany. There was talk of a "deal" with the Reich covering Samaná Bay. In early 1904 the Hague Tribunal handed down its ruling regarding special treatment for creditors who had used armed force to collect in Venezuela —an implied justification for debtor nations to do likewise in Santo Domingo. Morales was very shaky in the seat of power—he had few followers of his own. His collapse would probably be the signal for action by European states. France, specifically, announced that it planned to act. Roosevelt acted first.

After enunciating the Corollary in his annual message to Congress he told Secretary Hay to have the United States minister "sound the President of Santo Domingo, discreetly but earnestly and in a perfectly friendly spirit, touching the disquieting situation which is developing owing to the pressure of other governments. . . . You will ascertain whether the government of Santo Domingo would be disposed to request the United States to take charge of the collection of duties and effect an equitable distribution of the assigned quotas among the Dominican government and the several claimants."

Morales jumped at the opportunity to retain his position and have Big Brother straighten out his affairs. Roosevelt sent a special commissioner to Santo Domingo to make definite arrangements—with two warships to lend moral support. A protocol was prepared under which the United States agreed to help Santo Domingo work out of its financial crisis because the United States, according to the preamble of the protocol, viewed "any attempt on the part of the governments outside of this hemisphere to oppress or control the destiny of the Dominican Republic as a manifestation of an unfriendly disposition towards the United States."

In transmitting this protocol to the Senate, Roosevelt said: "Either we must submit to the likelihood of infringement of the Monroe Doctrine or we must ourselves agree to some such arrangement as that herewith submitted. . . . We . . . are simply performing in peaceful manner . . . part of that international duty which is necessarily involved in the assertion of the Monroe Doctrine. . . . This in reality entails no new obligation upon us, for the Monroe Doctrine means precisely such guarantees on our part. . . . This protocol affords a practical test of the efficiency of the United States government in maintaining the Monroe Doctrine."

The United States Senate refused to ratify the protocol. Roosevelt undertook some minor revisions. In the meantime he adopted a *modus vivendi* (in international law, a temporary arrangement pending final settlement) under which American agents controlled all customs houses, collected the revenue, allowed 45 percent to Santo Domingo and divided the rest among the debtors. It is interesting that Santo Domingo's 45 percent amounted to more money than had ever flowed into the treasury from the entire revenue when their own government did the collecting.

Although Morales was happy with this arrangement, his political opponents were not. Only the presence of American warships in Dominican waters made its execution possible. When signs of insurrection appeared late in 1905, Roosevelt sent a note to the Secretary of the Navy: "As to the Santo Domingo matter, tell Admiral Bradford to stop any revolution. I intend to keep the island in *status quo* until the Senate has had time to act on the treaty, and I shall treat any revolutionary movement as an effort to upset the *modus vivendi*. That this is ethically right I am dead sure, even though there may be some technical or red tape difficulty."

The United States, under a new interpretation of the Monroe Doctrine, had established a protectorate over the Dominican Republic, and established a precedent under which United States Marines would be busy "protecting" Latin American republics for more than a quarter century.

In extending the Doctrine to justify interference in the economic and political affairs of Latin American states, Roosevelt had come a long way from previous concepts of Monroe's message. But his basic purpose was the same as Monroe's. In his opinion the presence of any foreign warship in the Caribbean might lead to a situation in which "our rights" would be "invaded or seriously menaced." National security required the United States to take steps to prevent situations which might give cause for foreign fleets in the neighborhood of the canal.

Although he basically believed in imperialism, Roosevelt had no intention of annexing territory. And his was not "dollar diplomacy." He had little interest in the welfare of foreign or domestic bond holders—no President before him was so opposed to "the interests" or so detested by Wall Street. His creed was national security. The steps that he took to get it were direct and by his lights, proper. They were also effective—if not diplomatic.

But the Roosevelt Corollary ushered in the era of dollar diplomacy. His successor, William Howard Taft, and the new Secretary of State, Philander Knox, had a definite interest in the welfare of United States investments in Latin America. This is not to say that there was any dishonesty. But there was what would now be termed a very serious conflict of interest. For instance, one of the companies which benefited from United States intervention in Nicaragua was the United States and Nicaragua Company, which was largely owned by a family named Fletcher in Pittsburgh. Secretary Knox had been the attorney for the Fletchers. He and President Taft's brothers held stock in the company. Also, the Taft administration marked the beginning of a strong "community of interest" between the State Department and United States financial interests in Latin American affairs.

Nicaragua, at the time, was ruled by a dictator named José Santos Zelaya who was creating turmoil among his isthmian neighbors in an effort to extend his power to more of Central America. Among Zelaya's many faults was a dislike of Yankees, although he gave many profitable concessions to North Americans who were the highest bidders. In 1909 he took steps to refund the Nicaraguan national debt—in London. By this time foreign investments in the Caribbean area were frowned upon in Washington —and, of course, in Wall Street. A revolution broke out in 1909. There is good reason to believe that North American business firms in Nicaragua were behind it. When Zelaya executed two American soldiers of fortune, Washington immediately broke diplomatic relations, and, shortly after,

sent two warships and landed Marines to prevent government forces from entering the city of Bluefield and to keep
the ports open for the insurgents to receive arms and other
aid. With such help, the revolution was successful.

The leader of the revolutionists, General Estrada, became president. Adolfo Diaz became vice-president. Diaz
had been a bookkeeper in the mining company owned by
Knox's ex-client. The United States minister "suggested"
that Estrada resign. Diaz became president. He promptly
signed a treaty similar to the Santo Domingo pact which
placed the control of the Nicaraguan customs in North
American hands.

In submitting the Nicaraguan treaty to the Senate, President Taft sought the sanction of the Doctrine. "A further
responsibility is thrown upon us," he said, "by the Monroe
Doctrine. Much of the debt of Nicaragua is external and
held in Europe, and while it may not be claimed that by
the Monroe Doctrine we may be called upon to protect
an American Republic from the payment of its just foreign
claims, still complications might result from the attempted
forced collection of such claims, from the involutions of
which the government might not escape." When the Senate
refrained from promptly ratifying the treaty Secretary
Knox made another appeal in terms of the Doctrine in a
public speech in which he pointed out how well things
were going in Santo Domingo. He attributed this to the
Roosevelt Corollary which, he said, "had cured centuries
old evils." He said that "Mr. Roosevelt's Corollary would
diminish our responsibilities in proportion as we bring
about improved conditions. . . . It would not be sane to
uphold a great policy like the Monroe Doctrine and to re-

pudiate its necessary corollaries and neglect the sensible measures which reason dictates as its safeguards."

Although the Senate still refused to ratify the treaty, North American bankers agreed to loan Nicaragua $15,-000,000. American officials started to collect Nicaraguan customs, steps were taken to refinance the English loan in Wall Street, Yankees acquired control of the Nicaraguan bank and railroad, and most of the mineral rights of Nicaragua were in North American hands. In short, Wall Street was running Nicaragua through the pliant Diaz.

In 1912, when a serious revolution threatened to unseat Diaz, Marine Colonel Smedley Butler landed with two thousand men, and the protectorate was complete. The bellicose Butler led several of the Marine interventions in Latin America. Years later, when this salty, forthright Marine had retired as Commandant of the Corps he said, "I know that many of these expeditions were nothing but collection trips for the bad debts contracted by the Wall Street bankers."

Roosevelt's action in Santo Domingo *might* have been justified under the Monroe Doctrine. There was a real threat of European intervention which would have involved at least temporary control of territory in the Western Hemisphere by a foreign power. In Nicaragua no such danger existed, or was even rumored. True, there were some strategic elements involved. Zelaya was stirring up trouble in the neighborhood of the canal. But this was purely intra-American action. The Monroe Doctrine did not cover it—except in terms of the new interpretation under the Roosevelt Corollary.

After Nicaragua came Haiti, a problem for President Woodrow Wilson and his Secretary of State, William Jennings Bryan. In Haiti dollar diplomacy was a factor but, perhaps, not the primary cause for intervention. But the intervention could be justified only under the "policeman" concept of the Roosevelt Corollary.

To say that political affairs in Haiti were chaotic is a grievous understatement. From 1910 to 1915 there were six "presidents," each brought to power by a revolution. These were not popular uprisings. The revolutionary "troops" were bands of Haitian mercenaries called *cacos*, who made a living by selling their services to the man who would pay the most for their help in grasping the lucrative position that gave him control of the national treasury. There is evidence that some of these dusky politicians received the wherewithal to pay their supporters from German, French and private United States sources.

Foreign intervention in Haiti, on a very small scale, was quite common. There was frequently a warship of some nation—usually France—at Cap-Haiten, and when a revolution became too barbarous, Marines were briefly landed to protect all foreigners and restrict bloodshed. Financial interests were principally French and German, with France controlling the national bank. Haitian debts were badly in default. In 1909 France proposed to take over collection of the customs. The United States replied that it would "view with much concern" such an infringement of the Monroe Doctrine. When in that same year a German firm signed a contract with the Haitian government for a coaling station, the American State Department again frowned, ". . . Monroe Doctrine."

France and Germany kept pushing for international control of Haitian customs, with the United States participating. In response to a German proposal, President

Wilson replied with a strong note that detailed the current interpretation of the Monroe Doctrine saying, in part, "that the Government of the United States is well known to have taken for many years and without variation of policy the position that neither foreign mercantile influences or interests, nor any other foreign influence or interest proceeding from outside the American hemisphere could, with the consent of the United States, be so broadened or extended as to constitute a control, either in whole or in part, of the government or administration of any independent state. The government of the United States cannot depart from that policy, and feels confident that the Government of His Imperial Majesty will not expect it to do so."

In 1914 events in Haiti started to degenerate from the chaotic to the impossible. Between January of that year and February of the next there were four successive presidents. With each of them the United States tried to reach an agreement under which Haiti would promise not to cede Môle St. Nicolas to any foreign power and would accept United States supervision of the customs. Most of the presidents were willing to agree as to the Môle, but since having access to the country's revenue was the leading incentive to be president, none would agree to the latter provision.

In June, 1915, it seemed as though some progress was being made with the incumbent president, Vilbrun Sam. Then, another revolution broke out. In an effort to suppress it, Sam arrested every likely suspect, and the prison guard slaughtered them in cold blood. This barbarity led to a popular uprising. Sam was dragged from his refuge in the French legation, his body hacked to pieces, and the sections dragged through the streets. At this point the

U.S.S. *Washington* appeared in the harbor. Its landing force suppressed the revolution and took over. Within a few weeks the entire country was occupied by United States forces. A puppet government was set up and forced to sign a treaty granting customs control, a police force trained and manned by American officers and a promise never to lease or sell any of Haiti's territory to a third party.

Although the financial affairs of Haiti ended up in the hands of North American bankers, the occupation of Haiti was not solely dictated by dollar diplomacy. There were some possible grounds for fearing foreign intervention, but the main factor was the utter chaos that existed in the country. The situation was similar, in some respects, to that which prevailed in the Congo in 1960 when the United Nations intervened. Somebody had to do something about Haiti, which was sinking into complete savagery. There was no United Nations, so the United States delegated itself as policeman. But when the commanders of French and English warships on the scene offered to land forces to assist in suppressing the revolution, the American Admiral refused. An international police force was not allowable under the Monroe Doctrine.

In 1915 another interpretation of the Doctrine was put forward by Robert Lansing, who succeeded Bryan as Wilson's Secretary of State, in a memorandum entitled "Present Nature and Extent of the Monroe Doctrine." Previous to writing this he had made a proposal that "the Monroe Doctrine . . . should be restated to include European acquisition of political control through the agency of financial supremacy over an American republic. . . . Should a new doctrine be formulated declaring that the United States is opposed to the extension of European control over American territory and institutions through financial as well as other means?"

Wilson did not accept this proposal, under which the United States could have forbidden foreign loans to or concessions in Latin American countries. In Lansing's later, formal memorandum he modified this view somewhat, although still maintaining that European money was the root of much evil. He said that "a revolutionary chief finds little difficulty in financing his venture among foreign speculators in exchange for concessions and other privileges and the chance of large profits if the revolution is successful." This, he said, could lead to situations in which political domination by a foreign power could be acquired by "the subtlety of financial control. . . . To meet this danger the surest if not the only means is the establishment of a stable and honest government. . . . In order to accomplish this the first thing to do is to remove the prize of revolution, namely the control of the public revenues."

Lansing's memorandum concluded by saying, "It would seem therefore, that in the case of the republics about the Caribbean Sea the United States should expand the application of the Monroe Doctrine, and declare as a definite Caribbean policy that, while it does not seek domination over the territory of these republics, it is necessary for the national safety of the United States . . . that it aid the people of these republics in establishing and maintaining honest and responsible governments—and that it will not tolerate control over or interference with the political or financial affairs of these republics by any European power or its nationals."

Wilson accepted this memorandum "for the guidance and clarification of our own thoughts." He did not make it the basis of a public statement. But it is interesting that Woodrow Wilson, the great champion of democracy, was willing to accept any interpretation of the Monroe Doctrine designed to curb the freedom of neighboring states.

The era of dollar diplomacy lasted throughout the first thirty years of the twentieth century. This application of the Monroe Doctrine was never popular with the public. However, the people did not oppose it. They were simply not interested. American intervention was represented as being good for the people to whom it was applied. Figures were quoted as to how many schools and hospitals were built, how many miles of roads. American Marines brought law and order—freedom from the bloody barbarity of dictators and the evil schemes of foreigners.

In fact, the protectorates had "never had it so good" in terms of health, education and welfare. Economically, the people were at least as well off as they had been, if not better. But there was one thing that they did not have—independence. From 1915 to 1921 the United States Marines, and native troops under their control, killed three thousand Haitians. Many of these were the *caco* mercenaries, who were wiped out. But some of them were Haitian patriots fighting for freedom. The Monroe Doctrine, which came into being to guarantee the independence of the Latin American states, had been perverted to rob some of them of that independence.

9

Pan-Americanism and the Doctrine

The United States have deprived of their liberty the Philippines, Hawaii, Puerto Rico, Haiti and Santo Domingo, and have imposed upon the sovereignty of Cuba, Nicaragua, Honduras and Panama a political, military or economic slavery. The United States have seized from Colombia one of its provinces, and have invaded Mexico, occupying Vera Cruz by force of arms and a part of the northern frontier of the republic. These historical facts justify the title of this book: "The United States Against Liberty."

The above was the prologue to a book written by a respected Mexican diplomat during the height of the dollar-diplomacy era. Some of his "historical facts" are not historical. Puerto Ricans had no liberty to be deprived of, and Hawaiians were not only willing, but anxious, to be annexed to the United States. But it represents a Latin Amer-

167

ican view of the United States one hundred years after Monroe had propounded the Doctrine. An extreme view, perhaps, but not an uncommon one.

It had not always been thus. When Monroe delivered his message, all of Latin America was in accord with the principles that he set forth. In fact, many Latin American writers claim that Monroe was inspired by a South American. They point to a statement by Don Manuel Torres, a Colombian diplomat in Washington, who said, in 1821: "There has occurred a project, long since formed, to establish a monarchy in Mexico . . . to favor the views of the Holy Alliance in the New World. This is a new reason which ought to determine the President of the United States no longer to delay a measure which will naturally establish an American alliance capable of counteracting the projects of the European powers and of protecting our republican institutions."

Certainly the greatest of the South American liberators, Simon Bolivar, was fully in accord with the principles behind Monroe's message. A year after Monroe's speech he invited all of the Latin American states to a Congress at Panama. He told the delegates of his own country, "You shall see that the proclamation which . . . must be issued and published by the Great Congress of the Isthmus contains such an energetic and efficient declaration as that made by the President of the United States of America in his message to Congress of last year in regard to the necessity of the European powers of abandoning all ideas of further colonization in this continent, and in opposition of intervention in our domestic affairs. . . . You will endeavor to negotiate a treaty by which all of the new American states attending the Congress be united in a close alliance both offensive and defensive."

The last sentence of Bolivar's instructions points up the difference between the Latin American view and the Anglo-American view of effectuating the principles on which both agreed. Bolivar dreamt of, wrote about and worked for a confederation or league of American states, based on treaties and a covenant. The United States firmly believed in "no entangling alliances." In the few years following Monroe's speech Colombia, Brazil, Argentina and Mexico all asked the United States to agree to measures that would represent a mutual guarantee of independence. In all cases the United States refused.

Bolivar is often called the "father of Pan-Americanism." It would be more accurate to say that he wanted to be the father of Hispano-Americanism. Although all of his proposals for a league or confederacy did not exclude the United States, neither did they specifically include them. In his instructions above he said that the "new" American states should be united—the adjective did not apply to the United States. In fact, Bolivar was more interested in having Great Britain participate in the Panama Congress than the United States. He wrote a paper expressing his views on the Congress in which he emphasized the importance of England's presence and listed seven advantages to England, concluding with the statement that "the Panama Congress . . . may be the occasion for consolidating the new states with the British empire." This could hardly be called true Pan-Americanism.

When the Congress was held, in 1826, the United States did not participate. Although it had not been included in Bolivar's original invitation, it was later invited by Mexico,

Colombia and the United Provinces of Central America. The invitations made it clear that the Latin states wanted to "pluralize" or Pan-Americanize the Monroe message as the basis of a hemisphere agreement covering resistance to foreign intervention and colonization.

President Adams wanted to send delegates, although, he assured the Senate, "neither to contract alliances nor to engage in any undertaking or project importing hostility to any nation." He did, however, reiterate the views of his predecessor by saying that seven of the eight southern nations were "republics like ourselves; with whom we have an immensely growing commercial, and *must* have . . . important political connections; with reference to whom our situation is neither distant nor detached; whose political principles and systems of government, congenial with our own, must have an action and counteraction upon us and ours to which we cannot be indifferent if we would. . . . America has a set of primary interests which have none or a remote relation to Europe . . . and if she should interfere, as she may . . . we might be called, in defense of our own altars and firesides, to take an attitude which would cause our neutrality to be respected."

Although Adams' statement was clearly based on national self-interest, the Senate was not willing to accept even this concept of Pan-Americanism. It argued heatedly as to whether the United States should attend. The tenor of these long-ago debates laid the groundwork for United States-Latin American relationships for over a century.

There was no mention of the idealistic concept of a hemisphere of free and independent states where the rights of man would rule supreme. Rather the Senatorial schism was based on sectional commercial interests. While Adams, from Massachusetts, might see "immensely growing commercial connections" for the factories of New England, the agricultural states saw in Latin America nothing but a potential competitive producer of cotton and tobacco, wheat and cattle. The South had further reservations. Bolivar was a crusader against slavery, which had been outlawed in the Latin states.

The debates lasted for four months. Finally, since the commercial advantages might outweigh the disadvantages, the Senate grudgingly agreed to send delegates, but insisted that they be firmly instructed not to sign anything. One of the North American delegates died en route to Panama. By the time the other reached there the Congress was over.

The Congress of Panama accomplished nothing. It drew up a covenant for a league along the lines suggested by Bolivar, but the only country to ratify it was the Liberator's Peru. But the meeting did measurable damage to the absent United States. George Canning sent one of his most able diplomats, Edward Dawkins, to represent England and "avert the blow" struck by the Monroe Doctrine. Dawkins made much of the greater commercial advantages England had to offer, the superior strength of the British fleet as a guard against European interference, and flaunted the nonintervention promise that Canning had secured from France.

Later, Canning bragged of his agent's achievements in these words: "The great danger of the time . . . was a division of the world into European and American, Republican and Monarchial; a league of worn-out governments on the one hand, and of youthful and stirring nations, with the United States at their head, on the other. We slip in between. . . . The United States have gotten the start of us in vain; and we link once more America to Europe. Six months more—and the mischief would have been done."

Canning was wrong in his last sentence. The United States did not seek hemisphere solidarity under the Monroe Doctrine in six months—nor in one hundred years. At this time, and for long after, the primary interest in Pan-Americanism in the republic of the north was in terms of its own security—and wheher it was good for business.

The next meeting of Latin American states took place at Lima in 1847. Its occasion was the fear aroused by the expected invasion of General Flores for the purpose of re-establishing a monarchy in Ecuador with Spanish help. Obviously, this was a matter covered by the Monroe Doctrine. The United States was invited, but did not attend, although Congress did pass a resolution reiterating the no-colonization and nonintervention principle. There were other meetings of American states in 1856, at Santiago, and in 1864, at Lima. The United States attended neither. All of these meetings were primarily political: to consider matters of common defense and mutual protection. Since there was no mutality in the Monroe Doctrine the United States did no consider itself involved.

The first true Pan-American Conference was called by the United States in 1889 and was attended by all the independent states of the Western Hemisphere except the Dominican Republic. The United States concept of Pan-Americanism at that time is indicated by the seven-point agenda for the Conference. The first point dealt with "measures that shall tend to preserve and promote the prosperity of the several American states." The second covered a proposed customs union; the third, communications; the fourth, customs regulations and port charges; the fifth, uniform systems of weights and measures and patent, copyright and trademark laws; the sixth, a proposed common silver coin; the seventh, an agreement on a definite plan of arbitration. In short, except for the seventh point, the Conference was entirely devoted to commercial subjects.

The second Pan-American Conference, at Mexico City in 1901, was a continuation of the first. At the third, in Rio de Janeiro in 1906, the Latin American states wanted to talk about the forcible collection of public debts, a subject of keen interest at the time in view of recent developments in Venezuela and Santo Domingo. In 1902 the Argentinian Foreign Minister, Luis Drago, had addressed a memorandum to Washington dealing with this subject, which became known as the Drago Doctrine. It was occasioned by the blockade of Venezuela for the collection of debts from that country, and strongly opposed collection by force of arms, saying: "The collection of loans by military means implies territorial occupation to make them effective, and territorial occupation signifies the suppression or subordination of the governments on which it is imposed. Such a principle seems obviously at variance with the principles many times proclaimed by the nations of America, and particularly with the Monroe Doctrine, sustained and defended with so much zeal on all occasions by the United States, a doctrine to which the Argentine Republic had heretofore solemnly adhered."

The Latin American states at the 1906 Conference wanted to have the Drago Doctrine endorsed by the United States. Secretary of State Elihu Root, who briefly attended the Conference, avoided tying this subject up with the Monroe Doctrine and poured oil on troubled waters in a

speech in which he said: "We deem the independence and
equal rights of the smallest and weakest member of the
family of nations entitled to as much respect as those of
the great empire; and we deem the observance of that respect the chief guarantee of the weak against the oppres-
sion of the strong."

At the fourth Pan-American Conference, in 1910 at
Buenos Aires, the Monroe Doctrine became the subject of
a behind-the-scenes squabble among certain of the Latin
American states. This year had been accepted as the cen-
tennial of Latin American independence. Brazil, which
had been friendliest toward the United States of all the
larger southern countries, wanted to make this the occasion
of a testimonial to the United States expressing thanks for
the part that the northern republic had played in maintaining that independence. They had prepared a memorial
saying:

The long period that has transpired since the declaration
of the Monroe Doctrine permits us to recognize in it a permanent factor making for international peace upon the American Continent. For this reason, while celebrating her first
efforts for independence, Latin America sends to her Great
Sister Nation of the North, an expression of her thanks for
that noble and unselfish action which has been of such great
benefit to the entire New World.

This did not commit anybody to anything. It was
planned by Brazil merely as a gracious gesture of friendship. But several of the other states did not see it that way.
To them, the Monroe Doctrine had come to mean, at best,
the interfering big brother—at worst, the policeman with
the big stick. One of the Chilean delegates said, "More
than one country had felt its sovereign dignity to have been

wounded." After several efforts to amend the memorial so as to avoid seeming endorsement of the United States assumption of leadership and Yankee imperialism, the matter was dropped.

In 1911 another corollary was added to the Monroe Doctrine. Some American capitalists had acquired a large tract of land at Magdalena Bay in the Mexican province of Baja California. They proposed to sell it to a Japanese group. They discussed the project with the State Department and were told that if the Japanese government was involved the transfer would be in opposition to the Monroe Doctrine. When rumors of this proposed transaction reached the Congress it demanded information from the State Department—the "Yellow Peril" had raised its head.

Although the Japanese government categorically denied that it had any intention of acquiring the land, Senator Henry Cabot Lodge saw grave danger in such a situation and introduced a resolution that said, "When any harbor or other place in the American continents is so situated that the occupation thereof for naval or military purposes might threaten the communications or the safety of the United States, the Government of the United States could not see without grave concern the possession of such harbor or other place by any corporation or association which has such a relation with another government, not American, as to give that government practical power of control for national purposes."

The Senate passed Lodge's resolution by an overwhelming vote, and although the Senator from Massachusetts would not admit that his resolution related to the Monroe Doctrine, it was promptly dubbed a corollary to the Doctrine. The resolution said, in effect, that the United States claimed the right to interfere in the sale of land owned by private individuals in a Latin American state to other private individuals who were nationals of a European nation—a point of view that obviously was not very popular south of the Rio Grande.

A fifth Pan-American Conference was scheduled for 1914. It was delayed by the unsettled conditions of the First World War and did not meet until 1923. In the meantime, the Doctrine had occasioned another period of turmoil in connection with the League of Nations.

President Woodrow Wilson was an idealist—but his actions as President could not always be in accord with his philosophy. Although the policy of dollar diplomacy which he inherited from his predecessor was in direct opposition to his expressed principles, he did little or nothing to change it. Although he was the avowed champion of democracy, his administration was responsible for the intervention in Haiti, during which the Marines dissolved three democratic assemblies. Wilson further muddied Latin American relations by announcing that the United States would not recognize a government which came into being as a result of a revolution—a rather unrealistic position in connection with an area in which, for most states, revolution was a way of life. In this connection he intervened in Mexico and again offended Latin American sensibilities.

President Wilson was the first Chief Executive to strongly oppose the traditional United States policy of isolationism. He felt that only the moral leadership of the United States would "make the world safe for democracy," and before the United States entered World War I, he described to the Senate the kind of peace that the war must, in his opinion, bring about. Just as Theodore Roosevelt had sought to gain support from the sacred Monroe Doctrine to accomplish his purpose, Woodrow Wilson endeavored to use it to justify his point of view. He said:

I am proposing, as it were, that the nations should of one accord adopt the doctrine of President Monroe as the doctrine of the world; that no nation should seek to extend its polity over any other nation or people, but that every people should be left to determine its own polity, its own way of development, unhindered, unthreatened, unafraid, the little along with the great and powerful.

I am proposing that all nations henceforth avoid entangling alliances which would draw them into competitions of power, catch them in a net of intrigue and selfish rivalry, and disturb their own affairs with influences intruded from without. There is no entangling alliance in a concert of power. When all unite to act in the same sense and with the same purpose all act in the common interest and are free to live their own lives under a common protection.

The words "Monroe Doctrine" and "avoid entangling alliances" sounded familiar, but the statement "when all unite . . . in the common interest" was in direct opposition to United States policy since the birth of the country. A year later Wilson made his purpose more clear in the Fourteen Points which he set up as conditions of a proper peace. Most of these points had to do with internal European political affairs. Under the original Monroe Doctrine, which said, "Our policy in regard to Europe . . . is not to interfere in the internal concerns of any of its powers," these points were not the concern of the United States. The Fourteenth Point was, simply, "A League of Nations."

The United States entered the war. Eighteen months later Germany surrendered. Wilson went to Paris to guide a peace that would "make the world safe for democracy"

through a League of Nations. While he was negotiating
with the allies to develop a covenant for the League, opposition in the Senate started to roll, led by Republican
Senators Borah and Lodge. They based their attack on the
idea of a League squarely on Washington's Farewell Address, which called for two separate hemispheres, and on
the Monroe Doctrine.

Typical of the attack is this quotation from a speech by
Borah:

Why did we purchase the St. Thomas Islands [Virgin Islands]?
They were situated on one of the routes leading to the
Panama Canal. It was known or feared that Germany wished
to secure these islands. We would have no right to object to her
securing them except the right that arises out of the Monroe
Doctrine. As a sovereign nation Denmark had the right to sell.
As a sovereign nation Germany had a right to buy. Had she
purchased and had we submitted to it, the Monroe Doctrine
would have been at an end. Suppose she had purchased the
islands and had undertaken to take possession of them. Would
we have consented for Germany to have those islands on the
route to the Panama Canal? Would we have submitted to an
international court the question of whether or not we should
maintain the Monroe Doctrine? Or if we had submitted it and
it had been decided against us, would we have given up the
Monroe Doctrine and permitted Germany to acquire the islands? Suppose Germany had purchased them and had started
to take possession and we had moved our battleships to the
waters in the neighborhood of these islands to prevent her taking possession. . . . Under this league to enforce peace, that
would have put us in the wrong; and we would have found
ourselves a member of a league by the terms of which we invited all nations of Europe to fight us, because we refused to
submit the Monroe Doctrine to a tribunal or refused to give it
up. Do you think we would have submitted any of these questions to a tribunal composed entirely of foreign nations? If it

had been submitted, do you think the people of the United States would have sustained the treasonable administration that had done so?

While the storm brewed back home, Wilson worked out a covenant for the League in Paris, with some support from England and strong opposition from France. He returned to the United States with the first draft of the League's constitution, containing the highly controversial Article X, which read: "The High Contracting parties undertake to respect and preserve as against external aggression the existing political independence of all States members of the League. In case of any such aggression or in case of any threat or danger of such aggression the Executive Council will advise upon the means by which this obligation shall be fulfilled."

This, to the minds of the League's opponents, was a complete repudiation of the policy of Washington and the Doctrine of Monroe. Wilson proudly presented the Covenant to the members of both Congressional Foreign Relations Committees at a dinner at the White House. "What," said the frowning Senators, "will become of the Monroe Doctrine?" The President replied that it would not abrogate the Doctrine. The League would merely extend it to the world. The Doctrine was embraced in the League—no special reservation concerning it was necessary in the Covenant.

Two days later Lodge rose on the floor of the Senate to denounce this concept:

The Monroe Doctrine exists solely for the protection of the American Hemisphere, and to that hemisphere it was limited. If you extend it to all the world, it ceases to exist, because it rests on nothing but the differentiation of the American Hemi-

sphere from the rest of the world. Under this draft of the constitution of the League of Nations, American questions and
European questions and Asian and African questions are all
alike put within the control and jurisdiction of the League.
Europe will have the right to take part in the settlement of
all American questions, and we, of course, shall have the right
to share in the settlement of all questions in Europe and Asia
and Africa. Europe and Asia are to take a part in policing the
American Continent and the Panama Canal, and in return we
are to have, by way of compensation, the right to police the
Balkans and Asia Minor when we are asked to do so. Perhaps
the time has come when it is necessary to do this, but it is a
very grave step, and I wish now merely to point out that the
American people ought never to abandon the Washington
policy and the Monroe Doctrine without being perfectly certain that they earnestly wish to do so.

Borah and Lodge were Republicans, but even in his own
party Wilson was faced with a demand that there be something in the League Covenant that would preserve the holy
Doctrine. Wilson's Secretary of State, Robert Lansing,
feared that Article X would "permit European powers to
participate, if they could not act independently, in the
forcible settlement of quarrels in the Western Hemisphere." David Miller, the legal authority with the American delegation in Paris, said, "What the United States has
done, is doing and will do for Europe is enough, without
asking an unasked sacrifice of her interest and those of
Latin America, by giving up a policy which has prevented
the countries south of the Rio Grande from being, like
Africa, pawns in the diplomacy of Europe. . . . Beyond
doubt or question, the constitution of the League of Nations should contain an express recogition of the Monroe
Doctrine." Influential Democrat William Jennings Bryan

said that the United States "ought not to be asked to give up its paramount influence in the Western Hemisphere as a condition precedent to its entry into the League."

This comment of Bryan's is an interesting example of the lack of consistency which has always been associated with interpretations and applications of the Doctrine. While he was Secretary of State Bryan had negotiated a large number of bilateral "conciliation treaties." Eighteen of them were unanimously ratified by the Senate in one batch. All of these treaties provided that "the high contracting parties agree that all disputes between them, of every nature whatsoever . . . shall, when diplomatic methods of adjustment fail, be referred to an international commission." Obviously, "disputes . . . of every nature whatsoever" might include questions that were covered by the Monroe Doctrine. Although acceptance of an arbitrated decision was not binding in the Bryan treaties, the Senate which, in 1914, had unanimously accepted the principle of international arbitration refused, in 1919, to consider it unless questions covered by the Doctrine were excluded.

Wilson returned to Paris, still stubbornly opposing any amendment to the Covenant involving the Doctrine. But pressure on him increased—in cables from home, among his own delegation, and, strongly, from England. When he finally agreed to an amendment to Article X, the one he submitted was, with minor word changes, one that had been drafted by Lord Robert Cecil, the British delegate. It stated, "Nothing in this Covenant shall be deemed to affect the validity of international engagements such as treaties of arbitration or regional understandings such as the Monroe Doctrine." The French objected to this on the grounds that it weakened the participation of the United

States in the League. Also, said the practical French, if the Monroe Doctrine was involved in the Covenant it should be defined. Not so, said the English. They were opposed to a definition of the Doctrine that might "extend or limit its application." After all, they had their own vague "regional understandings," as in Arabia, which they were not anxious to formalize. After a night-long debate the proposed amendment to Article X was incorporated into the Covenant as Article XXI.

Article XXI by no means pleased the Senate. Both sides of the chamber introduced resolutions for reservations to this section, almost identical except in minor wording. The Republican resolution, drafted by Lodge, said that the Monroe Doctrine was "to be interpreted by the United States alone, and is hereby declared to be wholly outside the jurisdiction of said League of Nations." The Senate voted in favor of this reservation, together with fourteen others relating to different sections of the Covenant. Wilson refused to accept them and demanded unconditional ratification. The Senate refused to ratify, by a vote of 53 to 38. Wilson called for a "solemn referendum." He would take the matter to the people at the next election.

The Senatorial debates had not been entirely partisan. Although opposition to the League was led by Republicans, many Democrats crossed the aisle to vote with them. But in the campaign of 1920, the League was the big partisan issue. There is ample reason to believe that, until the political campaign started, the majority of the people favored some kind of a league of nations. The press reflected this opinion, and thirty of the state legislatures, as well as all the leading patriotic societies, had gone on record in favor of a league. But the Republicans hammered home that a vote for the Democrats was a vote against the sacred policy of George Washington and the holy Doctrine of James Monroe. Woodrow Wilson and the League of Nations were no match for this combination. The Republicans were swept into office and participation of the United States in the League of Nations was dead. The other powers ratified it and, subsequently, most of the Latin American states joined.

The debates on the Monroe Doctrine and the League were a further setback to Pan-Americanism. When Article XXI was incorporated into the Covenant there came cries from south of the border. What was this reference to the Monroe Doctrine as a "regional understanding?" Had not Wilson himself, at a Pan-American Scientific Congress in 1916, said, "The Monroe Doctrine was proclaimed by the United States on her own authority . . . it has always been maintained, and always will be maintained, on her own responsibility." To have an understanding, more than one party must be involved, and, certainly, no Latin American state was party to any understanding relative to the Monroe Doctrine.

Mexico, whose government was then particularly unfriendly toward the United States, expressed the extreme Latin American opinion. In commenting on Article XXI the Mexican Foreign Office said "that Mexico had not recognized and would not recognize the Monroe Doctrine . . . since it attacks the sovereignty and independence of Mexico and would place the nations of America under forced tutelage."

By the time that the fifth Pan-American Conference met at Santiago the United States had repudiated the League of Nations. As an alternative, for the Western Hemisphere,

Dr. Baltasar Brum, President of Uruguay, proposed an American League of Nations. He pointed out that the Monroe Doctrine had, for a century, prevented European conquests in the Western Hemisphere and that it was "the only permanent manifestation of the solidarity of one American nation with the others of the continent, "because it is the only one that has persisted throughout a century." Brum mentioned some of the criticisms of the Doctrine; it was "vexatious to the nations of America because it constituted something of a protectorate over them"; and aid from the United States "might wound the susceptibilities of the country . . . which would be protected."

The objections to the Monroe Doctrine could be overcome, claimed Brum, "if the American countries formulated a declaration similar to that of Monroe, binding themselves to intervene in favor of any one of them, including the United States, in case that one should, in defense of its rights, find itself involved in a war with some extra-continental nation. A declaration in this sense, incorporated into the international obligations of each country, would create for all a situation of great dignity, placing them on a footing of perfect moral equality with respect to the United States. . . . Thus, the Monroe Doctrine, proclaimed as a present standard of foreign policy only for the United States, would be transformed into a defensive alliance among all the American countries, founded upon a lofty feeling of solidarity, with repicrocal obligations and advantages for all of them."

Brum's proposal, the first cogent presentation of the idea of an Organization of American States, received short shrift at the 1923 Conference. The Colombian delegate attacked it violently. He spoke at length to list the instances on which the United States had failed to apply the Monroe Doctrine for the benefit of one or another of its neighbors, starting with the Falkland Islands. He agreed that it was necessary for the Latin American states to "organize the means of defense" against "every case of menace"—including, by inference, menace from the United States.

The United States delegation took no notice of this implied accusation. Its head, Henry Fletcher, merely said that time did not permit a discussion of the principles of 1823, but that the United States considered these principles "essentially national." Dr. Brum's proposed league was referred to committee, where it died.

This was Pan-Americanism at the centenary of the Monroe Doctrine. Some progress had been made. At least, the United States was talking to its neighbors—but mostly about customs, copyrights and other aspects of commerce. In matters of intercontinental political solidarity the United States stood alone. A formal Pan-American Union had been organized at previous meetings, with the Secretary of State of the United States as president. At the fifth Conference it was decided that the president of the Union should henceforth be elected, to reduce the influence of the United States. However, as a courtesy, they promptly elected the American Secretary of State.

Perhaps the best indication of the relationship of the Monroe Doctrine to Pan-Americanism was the refusal of the American delegation to discuss the Doctrine with its neighbors at a congress held in its century year. In the United States it was widely discussed. Secretary of State Charles Evans Hughes made two speeches at centenary celebrations which presented the then current definition of the Doctrine from the standpoint of the United States. He analyzed the Doctrine under six headings:

First. The Monroe Doctrine is not a policy of aggression; it is a policy of self-defense. . . . The achievements of the century have not altered the scope of the Docrtine nor changed its basis. It still remains an assertion of the principle of national security. . . .

Under this heading Hughes discussed the so-called Lodge Corollary and disassociated it from the Doctrine—without repudiating it.

Second. As the policy embodied in the Monroe Doctrine is distinctively the policy of the United States, the government of the United States reserves to itself its definition, interpretation and application. This government in asserting and pursuing its policy has commonly avoided concerted action to maintain the Doctrine, even with the American Republics.

Third. The policy of the Monroe Doctrine does not infringe upon the independence and sovereignty of other American States. Misconception upon this point is the only disturbing influence in our relations with the Latin American States. . . . We covet no territory; we seek no conquest; the liberty we cherish ourselves we desire for others; and we assert no rights for ourselves that we do not accord to others.

Fourth . . . So far as the Caribbean Sea is concerned, it may be said that if we had no Monroe Doctrine we should have to create one. And this is not to imply any limitation of the scope of the Doctrine, as originally proclaimed and still maintained, but simply to indicate that new occasions require new applications of an old principle which remains completely effective. . . . The Monroe Doctrine as a particular declaration in no way exhausts American right or policy; the United States has rights and obligations that the Doctrine does not define.

This section of the Secretary's speech went on to justify, at great length, the position of the United States in relation to Santo Domingo, Haiti and Cuba. He differentiated between the application of the Monroe Doctrine in the Caribbean and elsewhere in Latin America. He did not mention the Roosevelt Corollary—neither to associate nor disassociate it with the Doctrine. He talked much about the independence and sovereignty of the Latin American states —but he certainly did not repudiate the principle of United States intervention.

Fifth. It is apparent that the Monroe Doctrine does not stand in the way of Pan-American co-operation in the independence and security of American States.

Hughes went on to say that the five Pan-American Conferences had generated "helpful and friendly influences which draw peoples together through a better mutual understanding. . . . There is real progress in facilitating the interchange of commerce and culture." He listed the accomplishments of Pan-American Conferences in several areas. But on any proposed measures for political solidarity he said not a word.

Finally, it should be observed that the Monroe Doctrine is not an obstacle to a wider international co-operation, beyond the limits of Pan-American aims and interests, whenever that co-operation is congenial to American institutions.

In closing, the Secretary made a profound and prophetic forecast when he said:

The fact that intervention of non-American powers in this hemisphere is not threatened at this moment cannot be deemed to be controlling. The future holds infinite possibilities, and the Docrtine remains as an essential policy to be applied whenever any exigency may arise requiring its application. To withdraw it, or to weaken it, would aid no just interest, support no worthy cause, but would simply invite trouble by removing an established safeguard of the peace of the American continents.

Latin America did not view the Doctrine as Hughes interpreted it on its hundredth anniversary. They were willing, as they always had been willing, to accept the original premises—no colonization and nonintervention. They did not complain about such early modifications as the no-transfer principle. But Mr. Hughes had not withdrawn Mr. Olney's statement: "Today the United States is practically sovereign in this continent, and its fiat is law upon the subjects to which it confines its interposition." This blatant Yankee hegemony was an unacceptable part of the Doctrine to Latin America. Mr. Hughes had said nothing about Mr. Roosevelt's statement: "The Monroe Doctrine may force the United States . . . to the exercise of an international police power." No amount of explanation for the actions of the United States could make a Doctrine that embraced "the big stick" palatable.

Latin America as a whole resented both the big brother and the policeman. They resisted United States hegemony and feared Yankee imperialism—all of which they had come to associate with the Monroe Doctrine. And they strongly objected to the insistence of the United States that the Doctrine was unilateral; that "the government of the United States reserves to itself its definition, interpretation and application." None of the states south of the border were as strong as the United States; none, except Brazil, were as big. But, big or little, they were sovereign states and entitled to be treated as equals, not inferiors.

A statement representing the attitude of the larger southern states toward the Doctrine emanated from Argentina.

"The Argentine Republic will not be protected by Monroe's attitude because she has completed her evolution in civilization, and is now a respected country and knows how to merit the respect of the world. . . . We do not fear aggressions against our territory, either from Europe or from America, and there is not the slightest danger of our sovereign integrity being threatened by any nation whatsoever. Monroe's attitude is not, then, applicable to our country."

There was no true Pan-Americanism a hundred years after the Doctrine had been proclaimed, and Latin American-North Americans relations were to deteriorate still further, to reach an all time low at the sixth Pan-American Conference in Havana in 1928.

In 1925 United States Marines had left Nicaragua. Immediately, there was revolution. The United States refused to recognize the successful revolutionary government and sent back the Marines. There was another election, and with the help of a few Marines, Uncle Sam's good friend Adolfo Diaz moved back into the presidential palace.

Meanwhile, an intercontinental committee of jurists had been laboring, under the auspices of the Pan-American Union, to codify American international law. At a meeting in Rio de Janeiro in 1927 they reported out a draft of a code containing a clause that provided that "no state has the right to intervene in the internal affairs of another." This was placed before the Havana Conference in 1928 for consideration. Coming hard on the heels of the renewed interference in Nicaragua, it led to a violent eruption of anti-United States sentiment.

The head of the American delegation, Charles Evans Hughes, fluently defended the right of any state to "interposition of a temporary character for the purpose of protecting the lives and property of its nationals. . . . No country should forego the right to protect its citizens. International law cannot be changed by the resolutions of this Conference."

Hughes made his stand on the right of intervention— or "interposition," as he chose to call it—on the broad principles of international law rather than the Monroe Doctrine. But in Latin American minds the whole thing was squarely tied to the Roosevelt Corollary of the Monroe Doctrine. Although definite action on the proposal was avoided at the conference, thirteen states, led by Argentina, strongly supported the anti-intervention clause in the proposed legal code. The feeling was so intense that many observers felt that this was the end of the series of Pan-American Conferences. Conflicts were so deep-rooted that it would be useless to meet again. There were those who said that Pan-Americanism was impossible under the Monroe Doctrine. Certainly, it was impossible under the then current interpretation of the dogma and its corollaries. On the original principles behind the Doctrine there was complete agreement. The Doctrine could become the basis for a great advance in inter-hemisphere relations—if it could be Pan-Americanized.

In the United States a recognition of the need to modify the current concept of the Doctrine had been born and was maturing in a few obscure places—not in the Congress, the successive administrations, nor among the people, but principally in the colleges and the more thoughtful journals of opinion. As early as 1913 Professor Hiram Bingham wrote an article for the Atlantic Monthly entitled "The Monroe Doctrine: An Obsolete Shibboleth." Bingham claimed that the Doctrine had been modified to death. He vigorously attacked the right of intervention by the United States in the affairs of any Latin American state, pointing out that such intervention denied their right of independence—a fundamental right of every sovereign state. He said:

From the Latin American point of view the continuance of the Monroe Doctrine is insulting and is bound to involve us in serious difficulties with our neighbors. . . . If we still fear European aggression and desire to prevent partition of South America on the lines of the partition of Africa, let us bury the Monroe Doctrine and declare an entirely new policy. . . . Let us declare our desire to join with the "A B C" powers [Argentina, Brazil and Chile] in protecting the weaker parts of America against any imaginable aggressions on the part of European and Asiatic nations.

Bingham was the most outspoken North American critic of the Doctrine, but by no means the only one. No one else called it an "obsolete shibboleth" and proposed to bury it. But a survey among professors of international law disclosed that 104 out of 124 agreed with the principle of Pan-Americanizing the Doctrine to some extent. And this view was not confined to ivory towers—out of thirty-six newspaper editors queried, thirty held a similar view. Through the midde, 1920s when dollar diplomacy was still in vogue, a ground swell was forming that would lead to a new concept of Pan-Americanism, and a new era for the Doctrine.

10

The Doctrine
and the Good Neighbor

During the 1930s people in the United States, grouped around their radios, became familiar with an easy, drawling voice which addressed them as "my friends." President Franklin Delano Roosevelt always started his "fireside chats"—his informal reports to the people—with these words. And he frequently followed them with some homely talk about "good neighbors." Roosevelt was a genius at popularizing his ideas and his policies with down-to-earth, catchy labels. Foreign affairs became a "good-neighbor policy." The idea "love thy neighbor" was a lot more understandable to most people than the theory of Pan-Americanism. Under the good-neighbor policy the Monroe Doctrine received its most recent reinterpretation.

Originally, Roosevelt did not relate the good-neighbor

idea solely to Latin America. In his first inaugural address
he said that he would "dedicate this nation to the policy of
the good neighbor—the neighbor who resolutely respects
himself and, because he does so, respects the rights of others—the neighbor who respects the sanctity of his agreements in and with a world of good neighbors."

A year later Roosevelt enlarged on the meaning of the
good neighbor concept in Latin American relations when
he told the Pan-American Union:

> The essential qualities of a true Pan-Americanism must be the
> same as those which constitute a good neighbor, namely
> mutual understanding and, through such understanding a
> sympathetic appreciation of the other's point of view. . . . The
> Monroe Doctrine . . . was and is directed at the maintenance
> of independence by the peoples of the continent. It was aimed
> and is aimed against the acquisition in any manner of the con-
> trol of additional territory in this hemisphere by any non-
> American power.
>
> Hand-in-hand with this Pan-American doctrine of conti-
> nental self-defense, the peoples of the American republics
> understand more clearly, with the passing of the years, that the
> independence of each republic must recognize the independ-
> ence of every other republic. . . . Your Americanism and mine
> must be a structure built of confidence, cemented by a sym-
> pathy which recognizes only equality and fraternity. It finds its
> source and its being in the hearts of men and dwells in the
> temple of the intellect.

Although progress in Pan-Americanism was almost mi-
raculous during the Roosevelt administration, the groundwork for the change had been laid as far back as the last
years of Calvin Coolidge's sojourn in the White House,
and advancement in some directions had taken place during Herbert Hoover's term of office. Protests against the

misuse of the Monroe Doctrine from south of the border and in some quarters at home began to make an impression in Washington after the 1928 Havana Conference.

President Coolidge started to liquidate United States intervention in Nicaragua and Haiti, although the last of the Marines did not leave the former until 1932 and the latter until 1934. Woodrow Wilson's policy of not recognizing a revolutionary government was repudiated, except as to Central America. President Hoover made a goodwill tour of South America between his election and inauguration which at least indicated to the southern republics that the United States wanted to get better acquainted with its neighbors. Hoover also published an excellent memorandum on the Monroe Doctrine, which had been prepared at the instigation of his predecessor by Under Secretary of State Reuben Clark.

The Clark memorandum is the best and most recent analysis of the Monroe Doctrine and the nearest thing to an official declaration which the State Department has ever issued. After presenting a thorough historical background of the original Doctrine, Clark listed every application of it through the first century of its life, together with all of the interpretations, reinterpretations, corollaries and fallacies that had been associated with it. He stressed that the Monroe Doctrine was basically a policy of self-defense as applied solely to European attacks upon the Western Hemisphere which might be "dangerous to our peace and safety." Clark emphasized that the Doctrine "does not apply to purely inter-American relations. . . . The Doctrine states a case of United States vs. Europe, not of United States vs. Latin America."

The most significant section of Clark's paper had to do

with the Roosevelt Corollary. "The so-called Roosevelt Corollary," he said, "was to the effect . . . that in case of financial or other difficulties in weak Latin American countries, the United States should attempt an adjustment thereof lest European governments should intervene, and in intervening should occupy territory—an act which would be contrary to the Monroe Doctrine. . . . It is not believed that this corollary is justified by the terms of the Monroe Doctrine, however much it may be justified by the application of the doctrine of self-preservation." Although the United States did not, in 1930, entirely repudiate the principle of intervention, it did very definitely disassociate the big stick from the Monroe Doctrine and thus took one step toward the Pan-Americanization of the Doctrine.

Other steps followed in rapid order. At the seventh Pan-American Conference, held at Montevideo in 1933, the United States signed a *Convention on the Rights and Duties of States* which said: "No state has the right to intervene in the internal or external affairs of another state." True, they signed with a reservation as to the definition of "intervention," but this was a minor matter in relation to the renunciation of the principle. In 1934 the Platt Amendment was abrogated, freeing Cuba from United States interference. In another step the United States made a new treaty with Panama under which it gave up its right to intervene to assure Panamanian independence. This willingness to "soft pedal" auxiliary rights that had been claimed under the Monroe Doctrine was, in part, a serious change of front under the good-neighbor policy. Also, at the time, any threat of foreign intervention seemed remote.

By 1936 the situation had somewhat changed. The Fuehrer had rearmed Germany and marched into the Rhineland without opposition. Also the bitter and bloody Chaco War—a boundary dispute between Bolivia and Paraguay—had proved that the Western Hemisphere needed more effective machinery to maintain the peace. President Roosevelt called a special Inter-American Conference for the Maintenance of Peace at Buenos Aires, which he attended in person.

At Buenos Aires the nonintervention principle was re-affirmed—this time more definitely and without reservation by the United States. And another step was taken to remove the Latin American prejudice to the Monroe Doctrine. This was the *Convention for the Maintenance, Preservation and Re-establishment of Peace* which provided that "In the event that the peace of the American Republics is menaced, and in order to co-ordinate the efforts to prevent war," the American republics "shall consult together for the purpose of finding and adopting methods of peaceful co-operation." Further, the Convention provided that "In the event of an international war outside America which might menace the peace of the American republics, such consultation shall also take place to determine the proper time and manner in which the signatory states, if they so desire, may eventually co-operate in some action tending to preserve the peace of the American Continent."

Theodore Roosevelt's "big stick" was gone—the United States no longer claimed the right, under the Doctrine, to be a policeman. And Olney's contention that "the United States is practically sovereign . . . its fiat is law" was on the way out. At Buenos Aires the magic word "consultation" entered into hemisphere relations in connection with danger from abroad; although consultation was not yet mandatory, the Monroe Doctrine was starting to lose its purely unilateral character.

The eighth regular Pan-American Conference was held in Lima in 1938. By this time the march of the dictators was well underway, as was their efforts to bore from within in Latin America to spread the gospel of totalitarianism. Italy's Mussolini had conquered Ethiopia. Japan had invaded North China. Hitler had annexed Austria and dismembered Czechoslovakia. The Rome-Berlin Axis had been signed. Although there were many who hid their heads in the sand and hailed Britain's policy of appeasement toward Hitler, it was obvious to the clearer-thinking statesmen of the Western Hemisphere that danger from Europe was not as dead as it had seemed five years before.

The climate at the Lima conference was much improved for the progress of Pan-American solidarity. At Buenos Aires the principle of consultation had been approved, but no means had been established to effectuate it. The *Declaration of Lima,* adopted at the eighth conference, strongly reaffirmed the principle and set up machinery for putting it into practice. Also it stated the ideals which motivated Pan-American solidarity: "spiritual unity . . . unshakable will for peace . . . profound sentiment of humanity and tolerance . . . absolute adherence to the principles of international law . . . equal sovereignty of states . . . individual liberty without religious or racial prejudices."

After a preamble that set forth these idealistic concepts, the Lima Declaration listed four action points to assure their accomplishment. The signatory states reaffirmed their solidarity and their purpose to collaborate; they reaffirmed their decision to defend their principles and their sovereignty against all foreign intervention or activity that

might threaten them; they proclaimed "their common concern and their determination to make effective their solidarity, co-ordinating their respective sovereign wills by
means of the procedure of consultation"; they set up a
consultative procedure under which the Ministers for
Foreign Affairs of the American republics would meet,
"when deemed desirable and at the initiative of any one
of them."

Although the third point provided that "the Governments of the American Republics will act independently
in their individual capacity, recognizing fully their juridical equality as sovereign states," consultation was obligatory. The United States had renounced hegemony—its fiat
was no longer law.

Less than a year after the Lima Declaration was signed
Hitler marched into Poland to start World War II. Within
three weeks all of the Latin American states answered the
call of the United States to meet at Panama to consult on
measures to maintain the neutrality of the Western Hemisphere. The result was the demarcation of a neutrality
zone in the waters surrounding the hemisphere; an agreement to patrol the zone "individually or collectively"; and
a joint warning to the warring nations to refrain from com-
mitting belligerent acts in the zone. This was, in effect, the
first multilateral brandishing of the Monroe Doctrine
against threatened European aggression.

During all this progress toward hemisphere solidarity
during the 1930s, the Monroe Doctrine was seldom mentioned by name. It was called on neither to support nor to
justify the actions taken, nor was it claimed that the actions
violated or abrogated it. The United States did not formally announce that it was changed in any way. The

Doctrine still stood as Clark had described it in the memorandum which he wrote in 1928. Actually, it had been stripped of the three features which so incensed Latin America, and at Lima the other American states had accepted it in terms of its basic principles—something that they had been willing to do one hundred years before.

It was wise to keep the Doctrine in the background in diplomatic conversation. The words "Monroe Doctrine" were still offensive to Latin American sensibilities. But the failure to call on it or quote it in high places may have had a curious effect on pubic opinion in the United States. In a survey made by *Fortune Magazine* in the beginning of 1939 the question was asked "If a major foreign power actually threatened to take over any of the following places by armed invasion, would you be willing to see the United States come to the rescue with armed forces?" Only 43 percent of the people answered "yes" in connection with Mexico, only 27 percent in connection with Brazil. It would be interesting to know how much the percentages would have increased if the question had been reworded to say, "If a major foreign power threatened to violate the Monroe Doctrine by taking over, et cetera."

In 1940 the Doctrine again came to the fore. Hitler had overrun Holland. France had surrendered. The conquered European nations were in no position to deny the transfer of their colonies in the Western Hemisphere to Germany. French and Dutch Guiana, Martinique, Guadeloupe and the Dutch West Indies could become Axis bases threatening the American states.

The Monroe Doctrine made headlines in the press and was mentioned repeatedly in Congress as both Houses passed unanimously a resolution reiterating the no-transfer principle. The State Department sent a note to all belligerents saying that the "United States would not recognize any transfer and would not acquiesce in an attempt to transfer any geographical region of the Western Hemisphere from one non-American power to another non-American power." German Foreign Minister von Ribbentrop replied with a statement which attempted to twist the Doctrine to forbid American aid to the Allies. He said, "The nonintervention in the affairs of the American continent by European nations which is demanded by the Monroe Doctrine can in principle be legally valid only on condition that the American nations for their part do not interfere in the affairs of the European continent."

This European interpretation of the Doctrine was not new. Secretary of State Cordell Hull promptly scotched it with a note that disassociated the Doctrine from the European and Asiatic "sphere of influence" principle in which the strong dominated the weak. He said that the Monroe Doctrine "contains within it not the slightest vestige of implication, much less assumption, of hegemony on the part of the United States. It never has resembled, and does not today resemble, policies which appear to be arising in other geographical areas of the world, which are alleged to be similar to the Monroe Doctrine but which, instead of resting on the sole policies of self-defense and of respect for existing sovereignties, as does the Monroe Doctrine, would in reality seem to be only the pretext for the carrying out of conquest by the sword . . . of complete economic and political domination by certain powers of other free and independent peoples. . . . The United States pursues a policy of nonparticipation and noninvolvement in the purely political affairs of Europe. It will, however, continue to co-operate with all other nations . . . for the purpose of promoting economic, commercial and social rehabilitation, and of advancing the cause of international law and order."

After taking this unilateral position toward Germany under the Monroe Doctrine, the United States immediately called a meeting of the Foreign Ministers of the American states at Havana. Despite some objection from Argentina, which suspected that the United States had designs on the European colonies, the meeting adopted a measure for the *Provisional Administration of European Colonies and Possessions in the Americas.* This agreement provided that "When islands or regions in the Americas now under the possession of non-American nations are in danger of becoming the subject of barter of territory or change of sovereignty, the American nations . . . may set up a regime of provisional administration." This regime was to consist of a committee, with one member from each of the American states, which would administer the territory until "they are able to constitute and maintain themselves."

However, provision was made that unilateral action in this direction would be permissible under a clause which stated: "Should the need for emergency action be so urgent that action by the committee cannot be awaited any of the American republics, individually or jointly with others, shall have the right to act in the manner which its own defense or that of the continent requires." Although this specified that *any* state could take such action, its purpose was to free the hands of the United States to act alone—in short to apply the Monroe Doctrine unilaterally.

At this same meeting in Havana, a resolution introduced by Venezuela was adopted, without debate or fanfare, which was the most advanced step yet taken to internationalize the Monroe Doctrine. It said, simply: "That any attempt on the part of a non-American state against the integrity or inviolability of the territory, the sovereignty or the political independence of an American state shall be considered as an act of aggression against the states which shall sign this declaration." The pledge of hemisphere defense against foreign aggression was now completely mutual.

This pledge was soon tested by Pearl Harbor. When the United States was attacked nine of the Latin American countries immediately declared war on one or more members of the Axis. Four more promptly severed diplomatic relations. At a conference of Foreign Ministers called in Rio de Janeiro a month after Pearl Harbor all of the remaining southern states severed diplomatic relations except Argentina and Chile. Public opinion in Chile later forced a reluctant government to fall in line. Argentina, traditionally unfriendly toward the United States and ruled by a government which itself leaned toward totalitarianism, held out until 1944 and finally severed relations only under extreme pressure from the United States.

Paradoxically, the United States did not want the Latin American countries to declare war on the Axis. If they were belligerents the northern republic would be at least morally obligated to supply them with arms that were more needed eleswhere. What the United States did want—and what it got—was permission to establish bases where they were needed and an all-out effort from south of the border to supply scarce raw materials.

Every request for bases for antisubmarine patrol and air-ferry relay stations was granted. Few planes of the day could fly the North Atlantic with cargo. But they could fly the much shorter distance from the bulge of Brazil to the coast of Africa. Planes ferried over this route helped to stem the advance of General Rommel in North Africa and started the long allied advance which culminated in the invasion of Italy. In 1942 American armed forces were again in Latin America—guarding, at Brazil's request, a string of airfields, built by the United States with Brazilian co-operation, that stretched from the border of French Guiana to south of the bulge.

Normal sources of supply of many essential raw materials had been lost to Japan in the Pacific. Rubber production in Brazil was vastly expanded to replace imports from the Dutch East Indies. Manila fiber was grown in Mexico to replace the hemp of the Philippines. Eighty-three percent of the copper used in United States war production came from Peru and Chile. All of the quartz crystals used in optical equipment and all of the kapok used in life preservers came from Latin America. And it is possible that the island-hopping attack across the Pacific to Japan would have been slowed or stopped by malaria were it not for quinine made from the bark of cinchona trees in Mexico and Guatemala. These are but a few of the things for which the United States was completely dependent on its good neighbors to the south.

Although it is no part of historical reporting to speculate on what might have been, it is obvious that the reinterpretation of the Monroe Doctrine under the good-neighbor policy had much to do with the contribution of Latin America to the winning of the war. Under the Doctrine that existed in 1928 it is unlikely that the other republics of the hemisphere would have rallied so willingly to the support of the Colossus of the North.

Pan-American co-operation during the war was not all sweetness and light. There was criticism in the United States of aid that was being given to some southern states for nonwar projects. In Latin America the old distrust of their northern neighbor was easily rearoused by any ill-considered or thoughtless act on the part of the many North Americans who were stationed there. Argentina was a particularly thorny problem. She was unwilling to endanger her very profitable European trade in grains and meat by giving up her neutrality. Also, this most distant southern state had always been more closely tied to Europe than to the United States. Her temperate climate made her an agricultural competitor of the northern republic, which could not buy her grain and would not buy her meat. She was particuarly annoyed by a regulation forbidding the importation of Argentine beef into the United States. This was enacted because of the existence of hoof-and-mouth disease in some sections of the southern country, but its principal purpose was to protect the North American cattle and packing industries. There was an undercurrent of resentment on the part of some of the other Latin American states toward the pressure exerted by the United States to bring Argentina in line.

As the end of the war neared, the Latin American states feared that Pan-Americanism would retrogress in the postwar world. They were, perhaps, jealous that the United States seemed to be paying too much attention to the concept of One World at the expense of the welfare of the Western Hemisphere. This was borne out at the Dumbarton Oaks Conference, where the United States and the other major powers set up the broad framework for the United Nations. Here there was no talk of inter-American defense. The Latin American states were neither consulted about nor invited to Dumbarton Oaks.

Under pressure from south of the border an inter-American conference was held in Mexico City in 1945 at which the Latin American states expressed their views as to what kind of United Nations there should be. Their principal concern was for the sanctity of regional agreements. In 1920, when the United States insisted on an exception for the Monroe Doctrine in the Covenant of the League of Nations, calling it a regional agreement, the other American states had rebelled. In 1945, when it seemed that the United States would agree to a world-wide league which did not provide for a regional agreement that covered the same ground as the basic Doctrine, they again rebelled. This was a complete right-about-face. They wanted the message of Monroe, shorn of its later objectionable appendages, to continue to protect the Western Hemisphere. And they wanted the United States to take the lead. There was no talk, now, of the Yankee's horrible hegemony.

The meeting in Mexico brought forth the *Act of Chapultepec* in which the American states reaffirmed their belief in the importance of their regional system and drew up an alliance for the common defense for the duration of the war, after which it was to be replaced by a permanent treaty. This act went a step further than the declaration made at Havana in 1940. It covered aggression from an American state as well as a non-American state. At the time, this was aimed at Argentina, where the dictatorial government of Juan Perón had refused to co-operate in the war effort and seemed to be headed toward trying to impose its totalitarian concepts on its neighbors.

A month after the close of the Mexico City meeting the United Nations Conference on International Organization met in San Francisco. Here the Latin American states were represented in force. They accounted for 40 percent of the votes. With florid oratory—and allusions to the Monroe Doctrine—southern statesmen presented the case of regionalism vs. internationalism. The Dumbarton Oaks formula had called for a Security Council which would have total authority in deciding on action against an aggressor. No regional system could take action without permission from the Security Council. The Latin American States did not insist that a regional system be superior to the Council, but that it be independent of it in matters relating to self-defense within the area covered by the regional agreement. If the Security Council had supreme authority, foreign powers might intervene to impose their political systems in this hemisphere—a violation of the Monroe Doctrine.

It is interesting that the Latin American position was largely based on the fear of communism in some of the southern states—at a time when Russia and the United States were friends. Small groups of large landowners represented the "power behind the throne" in many of the American republics. Although they did not pine for the United States type of democracy, it was less of a threat to their positions than communism. They were the classic, traditional targets of Marx and Lenin. They wanted the United States to stand between them and the international revolution of the proletariat. Although this view was not publicly discussed in the presence of Russia's Vyacheslav

Molotov at San Francisco, it was an important factor in the behind-the-scenes negotiations.

The Latin American position was also influenced by Molotov's contemptuous attitude toward the smaller American republics at San Francisco. He considered them as merely satellites of the United States—that was the way his government treated weaker states and he could not understand a different system.

The strongest case for the principle of hemisphere defense—the original basis of the Monroe Doctrine—was made in a speech by the delegate from Colombia. After stating that his country had "confidence in the will for peace of the United Nations" he continued to say:

Colombia also believes that this system is a compromise . . . between the realities of 1945 and the aspirations of humanity. No American state can think otherwise because the inter-American system, functioning, of course, in a less complex continent, is unquestionably more perfect. The inter-American system proscribes all violence, all acquisition of territory by force, all intervention or interference of one country in the internal affairs of another, all aggression and, furthermore, unequivocally defines the aggressor. Should the latter appear on the scene, the Pan-American community would condemn it and apply sanctions by the democratic majority of its representative bodies; there is no privileged vote nor right of veto against such a desicion. In accepting a different and less perfect system we citizens of the Americas would not renounce our system; on the contrary, we would conserve the hope that the whole world might some day be ruled by the principles and procedures which have guaranteed peace, security, justice and respect to all our nations and which have permitted us to live unarmed. . . . No regional system like the inter-American one . . . can and should suffer any setback or detriment as long as, like ours, it shows that it is fully consistent with the aims of the general organization and, in addition, shows its efficacy in maintaining the peace and security of part of the world.

As a result of the strong stand taken by the other American states, who, on this occasion, led the United States, Article 52 was inserted in the United Nations Charter. It says, in part: "Nothing in the present charter precludes the existence of regional arrangements or agencies for dealing with such matters relating to the maintenance of international peace and security as are appropriate for regional action, providing that such arrangements or agencies and their activities are consistent with the Purpose and Principles of the United Nations." Thanks to Latin American insistence at San Francisco, there can be no Soviet veto of the Monroe Doctrine.

The next step toward hemisphere solidarity took place at Rio de Janeiro in 1947, where the *Inter-American Treaty of Reciprocal Assistance* was signed to give permanent status to the wartime measures adopted at Mexico City. The forward step here was a clause which provided that all decisions relative to action against an aggressor which were endorsed by a two-thirds vote of the signatory states were binding on all the states, "with the sole exception that no state shall be required to use armed force without its consent." Under this clause some aspects of United States foreign policy, short of war, could be determined by fourteen of its neighbors. Nothing could be further from the "United States fiat is law" principle which Olney had proclaimed a half century before.

The final flower of Pan-Americanism was reached in 1948 at Bogotá. Here the Organization of American States was born to supersede the Pan-American Union. To avoid confusion it should be explained that the Pan-American Union is still in existence as the General Secretariat of the Organization of American States.

The Charter of the Organization of American States is, in effect, a constitution for the Western Hemisphere. It outlines the ideals and purposes of the organization, the principles on which it is based and the rights and duties of the member states. In general terms, it outlines the major functions of the organization: the peaceful settlement of disputes; collective security; and economic and cultural development—although each of these functions is spelled out in greater detail in separate agreements.

The preamble of the Charter, and the sections of it dealing with inter-American political relations and Western Hemisphere security are important in connection with an understanding of the modern Monroe Doctrine. The preamble stated:

IN THE NAME OF THEIR PEOPLES, THE STATES REPRESENTED AT THE NINTH INTERNATIONAL CONFERENCE OF AMERICAN STATES, Convinced that the historic mission of America is to offer to man a land of liberty, and a favorable environment for the development of his personality and the realization of his just aspirations;

Conscious that that mission has already inspired numerous agreements, whose essential value lies in the desire of the American peoples to live together in peace, and, through their mutual understanding and respect for the betterment of all, in independence, in equality and under law;

Confident that the true significance of American solidarity and good neighborliness can only mean the consolidation on this continent, within the framework of democratic institutions, of a system of individual liberty and social justice based on respect for the essential rights of man;

Persuaded that their welfare and their contribution to the progress and the civilization of the world will increasingly require intensive continental co-operation;

Resolved to persevere in the noble undertaking that humanity has conferred upon the United Nations, whose principles and purposes they solemnly affirm;

Convinced that juridical organization is a necessary condition for security and peace founded on moral order and on justice;

HAVE AGREED UPON THE FOLLOWING CHARTER OF THE ORGANIZATION OF AMERICAN STATES.

ARTICLE ONE

The American States establish by this Charter the international organization that they have developed to achieve an order of peace and justice, to promote their solidarity, to strengthen their collaboration, and to defend their sovereignty, their territorial integrity and their independence. Within the United Nations, the Organization of American States is a regional agency.

Most of the one hundred and eleven articles of the Charter deal with organizational structure and matters such as inter-American economy, human welfare, education, cultural relations and law. Among the articles that set the pattern for inter-American political relations and hemisphere defense are the following:

The American States condemn war of aggression: victory does not give rights.

Controversies of an international character arising between two or more American States shall be settled by peaceful procedures.

States are juridically equal, enjoy equal rights and equal capacity to exercise these rights. The rights of each state depend not upon its power to ensure the exercise thereof, but upon the mere fact of its existence as a person under international law.

The fundamental rights of States may not be impaired in any manner whatsoever.

The political existence of a State is independent of recognition by other States.

The jurisdiction of States within the limits of their national territory is exercised equally over all the inhabitants, whether nationals or aliens.

No State or group of States has the right to intervene, directly or indirectly, for any reason whatsoever, in the internal or external affairs of any other State. The foregoing principle prohibits not only armed force but also any other form of interference or attempted threat against the personality of the State or against its political, economic and cultural elements.

No State may use or encourage the use of coercive measures of an economic or political character in order to force the sovereign will of another State and obtain from it advantages of any kind.

The territory of a State is inviolable; it may not be the object, even temporarily, of military occupation or of other measures of force taken by another State, directly or indirectly, on any grounds whatever. No territorial acquistions or special advantages obtained either by force or by other means of coercion shall be recognized.

The American States bind themselves in their international relations not to have recourse to the use of force, except in the case of self-defense in accordance with existing treaties or in the fulfillment thereof.

Every act of aggression by a State against the territorial integrity . . . or against the sovereignty or political independence of an American State shall be considered an act of aggression against the other American States.

If the inviolability or the integrity of the territory or the sovereignty or political independence of any American State should be affected by an armed attack or by an act of aggression that is not an armed attack, or by an extra-continental conflict, or by a conflict between two or more American States, or by any fact or situation that might endanger the peace of America, the American States, in furtherance of the principles of continental solidarity or collective self-defense, shall apply the measures and procedures established in the special treaties on the subject.

Thus, at mid-twentieth century, Simon Bolivar's dream of a league of American States came true. All of the basic principles of Monroe's message are made explicit by the Charter—although it goes much further, in that it provides not only for defense against European aggression but against inter-American aggression or intervention as well. Yet, there is a paradox. Although the Monroe Doctrine is embraced in the Charter, it exists independently of the Charter as well.

11

The Doctrine and the Ideologies

We all know that armed force is not the only instrumentality by which nations can be conquered. Equally, the dissemination by nations of doctrines and the carrying on of other types of activity can be utilized for the purpose of undermining and destroying in other nations established institutions of government and basic social order. . . . There is no place in the Western Hemisphere for . . . such doctrines and theories.

Secretary of State Cordell Hull said that in 1938. He was not talking, then, about communism. The threat was from the Fascist Fifth Columns that were active in all the southernmost states of South America. Adolf Hitler is supposed to have said, in a breezy moment, "I can take Brazil whenever I want to—by telephone." He did say, regarding South America, "We shall create a new Germany there. We shall find everything we need there. . . . We shall not land troops like William the Conqueror and gain Brazil by force of arms. Our weapons are not visible ones."

Statistics vary as to how many Germans resided in Latin America. There were allegedly two million in Brazil alone, many of them concentrated in the area where Brazil, Argentina and Uruguay meet. They spoke German, their children went to German schools and studied from German textbooks. There were signs in the street saying, "Unser land is ein stuck von Deutschland" (Our land is part of Germany).

By the end of 1938 German propaganda was in full flower south of the border. There were art exhibits in German cultural clubs, free beer in German sports clubs. Theaters played subsidized German movies instead of the more expensive Hollywood product. The land was blanketed with short-wave German propaganda broadcasts. Some of the most influential newspapers were German owned, and Germany supplied all papers with an excellent news and picture service extolling German love and friendship for Latin America.

In some countries the military was honeycombed with Nazis. Both the Peruvian and Chilean armies were German trained. In Argentina the young officers who backed dictator Juan Peron dreamed of gaining back the territories of its neighbors that had been part of the original Spanish colony, just as Hitler had reunited Austria and the Sudetan area of Czechoslovakia into a Greater Reich.

Before the end of the 1930s Germany had become the most influential European country commercially in the southern part of the continent. She was the leading exporter to Brazil and Chile, almost tied for first place with England in Argentina. And most German businessmen were Nazi propagandists or agents, including many who worked for United States firms. Germany virtually controlled the commercial airlines of South America.

A *putsch* of the Nazi "Green Shirts" was nipped in the bud in Brazil in 1938. When a planned uprising in Uruguay was discovered, Brazil mobilized troops on the border, and the United States sent a cruiser to Montevideo. Although the cloak-and-dagger aspect of Nazi activities in Latin America was exaggerated, the inherent danger was very real. Through these methods Germany annexed Austria without firing a shot and conquered Norway with but a slight military effort.

The Monroe Doctrine clearly opposed the introduction of totalitarianism or communism into the Western Hemisphere from abroad. These were European political systems, and Monroe had said, "We should consider any attempt on their part to extend their system to any portion of this hemisphere as dangerous to our peace and safety." Conquest by ideology was not new—witness the spread of Christianity. But political domination based on propaganda backed up by subversion was a new type of aggression to which the Doctrine had never been applied.

It was not applied against the Nazi ideology. By 1938 the danger was recognized and combatted, under the good-neighbor policy, with diplomacy, economic aid and counterpropaganda. Except for Argentina, where Nazi agents remained active until late in the war, the Fifth-Column threat was overcome by each of the Latin American states after they broke relations with the Reich.

After the war the ideological danger shifted to communism, although the United States was slow to appreciate it. Russia had been a brave ally in the war. Her insistence on the Security Council veto in the United Nations

Charter should have been a tip-off that she did not intend to renounce aggression as a national policy, but it was not until the end of the 1940s that the United States realized the extent of the threat, and then not immediately in connection with Latin America.

There are almost as many viewpoints about communism in Latin America as there are Latin American experts. There have always been some who claimed that the area is a natural target for the Kremlin. Widespread poverty coupled with a high rate of illiteracy form a breeding ground for communism. The maldistribution of land is a favorite target of communist propaganda—and the large landowner is a symbol of Latin America. In Peru, for instance, ninety percent of the arable land is owned by two percent of the people. The dormant fear of United States domination and "Yankee imperialism" gives a system in opposition to the United States added appeal.

There is another opinion which, until recently, tended to minimize the threat of communism south of the border. Experts in this camp pointed out that the Latin American is not temperamentally suited to accept communism. Like his northern neighbors, he considers independence and freedom as his heritage. And there are other factors which operate against communism: the Catholic church; economic dependence on the United States; and the political importance of the military leaders who are, generally, ardent nationalists.

In the most recent book on the Monroe Doctrine, written by Dexter Perkins, the outstanding authority on the subject, and published in 1955, the writer said: "There seems little doubt that communism has been on the retreat since the end of the war. Naturally it throve during the

period when the Soviet Union was the associate of the
American states in the struggle against Hitler. It showed
many signs of vitality in the period that immediately followed . . . but today the situation is by no means as favorable." He continued to point out that at least eleven of the
twenty Latin American states had declared the Communist
Party illegal—including Cuba.

Where revolution is accepted as a method of political
change, the outlawing of a party does not mean its permanent suppression. It may well come into power with the
next revolution. In any event, since Cuba embraced the
Kremlin in 1960, any discussion of the likelihood of violating the Monroe Doctrine by the establishment of a
foreign system in the Western Hemisphere through ideological means is purely academic.

The United States took the first definite diplomatic
action to combat communism in Latin America in 1954.
At the tenth Inter-American Conference at Caracas it secured the passage of a resolution stating that "The domination or control of the political institutions of any American
State by the international communist movement extending
to this hemisphere the polticial system of extra-continental
power would constitute a threat to the sovereignty and
political independence of the American States, endangering the peace of America."

Secretary of State John Foster Dulles felt that this was
another step forward in Pan-Americanizing the Monroe
Doctrine. "It seemed to me," he said, "as I planned for the
Caracas conference, that the threat which stems from international communism is the same kind of danger against
which President Monroe had made his famous declaration
one hundred and thirty years ago. It seemed of the utmost

importance that, just as a part of the Monroe Declaration had long since been turned from a unilateral declaration to a multilateral declaration of the American States, so it would be appropriate for the American States to declare the danger to them all which would come if international communism seized control of the political institutions of any American State.

The declaration was adopted by the Organization of American States with but one dissenting vote—Guatemala—and two abstentions, Argentina and Mexico. But there is a great difference between a multilateral declaration and united action. When Fidel Castro marched down from the mountains of Cuba to oust the tyrannical Batista he was hailed as a liberator. Here was a man of the people who would bring democracy to the Pearl of the Antilles. His government was immediately recognized by the other American States. The United States accepted at face value his statement that free elections would be deferred temporarily until things settled down.

It soon started to become apparent that Castro would not be a good neighbor in the democratic tradition. Widespread political executions of opponents on the grounds that they were enemies of the state smacked of the most brutal dictators, or of a Russian purge. Hysterical, rabble-rousing accusations against the United States were poured forth in marathon televsion speeches. A notorious Communist was appointed to head the Cuban National Bank. He stopped payment on $80,000,000 worth of American oil, and when British and American refineries in Cuba refused to process Soviet oil, Cuba expropriated the properties. When the United States retaliated by cutting the Cuban sugar quota, Castro pledged the island's sugar crop to Russia in return for economic aid, technical assistance and "defensive" armaments. By 1960 Cuba had willingly become a Soviet satellite—Castro had dropped this Western Hemisphere plum into a delighted Khrushchev's lap.

This was obvious to the United States. Other American states took a different view. Castro claimed that his government represented Cuban socialism, not international communism. His free country had a right to throw off the economic yoke of the Yankee and trade where it pleased. Throughout Latin America there was a good deal of sympathy for the bearded David who was defying the colossal Goliath. Mexico's President, Adolfo Lopez Mateos, said that he did not consider Cuba a threat to hemisphere peace and that his country had no obligation "to help the United States enforce the Monroe Doctrine."

The next semiofficial reference to the Monroe Doctrine in connection with Cuba came not from the United States but from Russia. A Russian reporter set the stage for Khrushchev to sound off against the Doctrine at a press conference by saying, "Various American bourgeois press organs contend that the development of friendly relations between the Soviet Union and Cuba represents open disregard for the so-called Monroe Doctrine. Our readers would like your opinion on this question."

The Soviet Premier was glad to give his opinion. He paid tribute to the Monroe Doctrine and the "positive role of United States foreign policy" one hundred and thirty seven years ago. But later, he said, "everything changed abruptly. Now the United States is using the Monroe Doctrine to substantiate a right to rule all American countries, meddle in their domestic affairs, keep them under its tutelage and, of course, exploit them." Today, he continued, "it is Marxism-Leninism . . . that is flourishing. . . . We consider that the Monroe Doctrine has outlived its time . . . has died, so to say, a natural death. Now the remains of this doctrine should best be buried as every dead body is so that it should not poison the air by its decay."

The State Department answered Khrushchev by saying that "the principles of the Monroe Doctrine are as valid today as they were in 1823 when the Doctrine was proclaimed. . . . The principles which the United States enunciated in the face of the old imperialism to intervene in the affairs of this hemisphere are as valid today for the attempts of the new imperialism. It consequently reaffirms with vigor the principles expressed by President Monroe."

In April, 1961, the State Department issued a "White Paper" condemning the Castro regime in Cuba, not because the government was established by revolution, but because "the leaders of the revolutionary regime betrayed their own revolution . . . into the hands of powers alien to the hemisphere" and converted it "into a mechanism . . . for the seizure, by international communism, of a base and bridgehead in the Americas and for the destruction of the inter-American system. It is the considered judgment of the government of the United States of America that the Castro regime in Cuba offers a clear and present danger to . . . the Americas."

Here was clearly a situation which called for multilateral action by the Organization of American States in accordance with the Caracas declaration of 1954 and a similar resolution that had been adopted, by a vote of 19 to 0, in San Jose, Costa Rica, in August, 1960. At a meeting of the American states called at Punta del Esta, Uruguay, in January, 1962, Secretary of State Dean Rusk introduced a resolution declaring that the Cuban regime was incompatible with the inter-American system and providing that Cuba should be excluded from inter-American organizations; all hemisphere trade with Cuba should cease; a special security committee should be established to study measures against aggression from the Soviet bloc.

The resolution was adopted by fourteen members—the necessary two-thirds majority. But its acceptance was, actually, a defeat for the United States. Cuba voted against it, of course, and six important states abstained from voting: Argentina, Brazil, Chile, Mexico, Bolivia, and Ecuador. They were willing to agree to declarations that international communism was a threat to the hemisphere, in theory, but, in practice, they sought to evade action by claiming that the Castro regime and international communism were not synonymous.

In all of this the Monroe Doctrine was not mentioned, officially, except in reply to Khrushchev's press conference. Unofficially, it had been brought out of moth balls and was widely waved and publicly proclaimed in the United States. The popular feeling seemed to be that consultation was fine, but if the Monroe Doctrine was being violated the United States should do something. Almost all newspapers and magazines of opinion editorialized on it. A quotation from *The New York Times* is typical. "Former Vice President Nixon, in the name of the Monroe Doctrine, calls for a quarantine of the island. A number of Congressmen invoking the Doctrine advocate military intervention under one or another guise. Congressional resolutions based on the Monroe Doctrine declare that it is the intent of the United States to employ force if necessary to protect our interests in the Caribbean and to prevent the export of communism from Cuba. Columnists, some sober, others frantic, fall back upon the Monroe Doctrine in their appeals that something be done about Cuba. For if the Monroe Doctrine is not relevant to the flagrant Soviet intervention in Cuba, to what conceivable set of circumstances can it be relevant?"

On October 21, 1962, the White House announced that President John Kennedy would take to the air the next day to deliver an important message to the country. The subject was shrouded in secrecy. At the appointed hour the President announced, in a short speech, that air reconnaissance photographs had disclosed intermediate-range missiles in Cuba capable of delivering an atomic warhead to Washington, Mexico City, or any part of Central America. Bases for longer-range missiles, that could strike any part of the Western Hemisphere, were under construction. This, said President Kennedy, "constitutes an explicit threat to the peace and security of all the Americas. . . . We no longer live in a world where only the actual firing of weapons represents a sufficient challenge to a nation's security and of the entire Western Hemisphere, and under the authority entrusted to me by the Constitution as endorsed by the resolution of the Congress I have directed that the following initial steps be taken immediately."

The principal steps were a quarantine of Cuba by the United States Navy to prevent the landing of further arms, and the concentration of Army and Air Force units on the coast of Florida in a state of maximum readiness.

President Kennedy continued: "It shall be the policy of this nation to regard any nuclear missile launched from Cuba against any nation in the Western Hemisphere as an attack by the Soviet Union on the United States requiring a full retaliatory response upon the Soviet Union. . . . We are calling tonight for an immediate meeting of the organization of consultation under the Organization of American States to consider this threat to hemisphere security. . . . Under the Charter of the United Nations we are asking tonight that an emergency meeting of the Security Council be convoked without delay to take action against the Soviet threat to world peace. . . . This nation is prepared to present its case against the Soviet threat to peace and our own proposals for a peaceful world at any time and in any form—in the Organization of American States, in the United Nations, or in any other meeting that could be useful without limiting our freedom of action."

The Organization of American States unanimously endorsed the action of the United States the next day. While the matter was under discussion in the United Nations, Khrushchev agreed to withdraw the offensive missiles and long-range bombers from Cuba.

President Kennedy did not mention the Monroe Doctrine. But his action was the most forceful employment of the Doctrine in the one hundred and thirty-nine years since President Monroe made his speech. Never before had the United States mobilized its armed forces with loaded guns and sent its Navy to sea with orders to shoot in defense of the principles enunciated by Monroe.

The Cuban situation, and the action taken, clarifies much in connection with the position of the Monroe Doctrine today. Before Cuba became a Communist satellite there were many who said—as it had so often been said in the past—that the Monroe Doctrine was dead. This time they seemed to say it with more reason. In the day of intercontinental missiles, hemisphere defense, they claimed, was an outmoded principles; defense should be planned in global terms. Also, they said, the United States had foresworn the Monroe Doctrine under the Charter of the Organization of American States; in the inter-hemisphere treaties and declarations of the 1930s and 40s the United States had renounced its right to apply the Monroe Doctrine.

The Doctrine has been dormant for the last forty years—but hibernation is not death. There are several reasons why it was not brandished so arrogantly as in the latter part of the nineteenth century and the early years of the twentieth. There were few occasions on which it needed to be awakened. And United States diplomats have become more sophisticated—or less adolescent—in their pronouncements. But the main reason that less has been heard of the Doctrine is the realization, on the part of the United States Government, that the words "Monroe Doctrine" are nasty words to Latin American ears. Connoting, as it does, the era when the Doctrine was used to justify Yankee imperialism, dollar diplomacy and intervention in the internal affairs of the smaller states, the title of the sacred dogma is best avoided in inter-American negotiations. In a collection of all the important diplomatic papers and speeches dealing with Pan-Americanism, published in 1955, the words "Monroe Doctrine" are not used in any speech or document more recent than Franklin Roosevelt's "Good Neighbor" speech of 1933.

On the last two occasions when the principle of the Doctrine was applied—in 1940 to Germany and in 1962 to Russia—the United States did not mention the Doctrine by name. It is curious that, in 1940, it was Germany which referred to the Doctrine in connection with the non-transfer of colonies, and in 1962 it was Russia which first publicly referred to it by name. Although Khrushchev blustered that it was dead, he was certainly very conscious of its existence.

In both instances where the Doctrine has been applied—in fact, if not by name—since the Organization of American States was formed, it was applied unilaterally by the United States. In both cases the procedure was the same. The United States first took its stand, alone, in applying the principles of the Doctrine and then called upon its neighbors to endorse that stand. In each case the endorsement was unanimous.

This is why it may be said that the Doctrine of today is embraced within the Pan-American system, yet exists independently of it. The United States has never given up its right to apply the Doctrine unilaterally, and nothing in any inter-hemisphere or international agreement denies them this right. Under international law the right to act in self-defense is an undeniable privilege of every sovereign state. Article 51 of the Charter of the United Nations recognizes this by saying, "Nothing in the present Charter shall impair the inherent right of individual or collective self-defense if an armed attack occurs against a member of the organization."

The words "armed attack" are subject to interpretation in specific cases. Reuben Clark, in his memorandum defining the Monroe Doctrine, said, "There is a broad domain occupied by self-preservation which is incapable of definite boundary as to its extent, or of definition as to the kind of act which lies within it, because new conditions, new advances in the arts and sciences . . . new political theories and combinations vary from age to age and cannot be foretold." President Kennedy pointed out that "We no longer live in a world where only the actual firing of weapons represents a sufficient challenge to a nation's security to constitute maximum peril."

The Monroe Doctrine is and always has been, when properly interpreted, solely a measure of self-defense for the United States. Monroe said it applied "only when our rights are invaded or seriously menaced." Every statesman since Monroe has reiterated the defensive character of the Doctrine—although, under the Roosevelt Corollary, there were some strange interpretations of self-defense. In the nearest thing to an official interpretation of the Doctrine ever issued by the State Department, Reuben Clark summed it up by saying, "It must not be overlooked that the matters inhibited by the Doctrine came under ban because they were 'dangerous to our peace and safety' or were a 'manifestation of an unfriendly disposition toward the United States' or 'endangering our peace and happiness.' "

President Kennedy's action in the Cuban situation indicates how the Doctrine lives side by side with international agreements. First he announced that the United States would act against a foreign threat to peace. Then he said, "This nation is prepared to present its case . . . at any time or in any form . . . in any meeting that could be useful *without limiting our freedom of action.*" In applying the modern Monroe Doctrine the United States seeks the support and co-operation of its southern neighbors and is very concerned about a united front in the Western Hemisphere. But, in so doing, the United States does not give up any of the rights which the Doctrine was designed to guard.

The point of view that the old concept of two hemispheres is outmoded in a day of one world, and that the

Doctrine is therefore obsolete, is definitely denied by the situation in Cuba. The matter of global defense involves questions of military strategy that are beyond the understanding of the layman. But, regardless of advances in weaponry, a potential enemy ninety miles away is obviously more dangerous than one three thousand miles away. It is true that, since the oceans are no longer so important as defensive barriers, the United States cannot limit the area in which its security can be threatened to the Western Hemisphere. But, in the words of Monroe's message, "With the movements in this hemisphere we are, of necessity, more imediately connected."

The Monroe Doctrine does not loom so large today in the over-all picture of United States defense as it did in the last century. But that does not mean that it is no longer valid or necessary. It is the basis of the regional agreement embodied in the Charter of the Organization of American States. Such regional agreements are important blocks in the wall of national defense. NATO and SEATO are also regional agreements covering other areas, but they do not replace the Monroe Doctrine as the policy that protects the all-important area nearest home.

The validity of the Doctrine today may, perhaps, be best understood by considering the closing paragraph of Reuben Clark's memorandum in the light of current dangers. The interpretative memorandum said:

The Doctrine does not concern itself with purely inter-American relations; it has nothing to do with the relationship between the United States and other American nations, *except where other nations shall become involved with European governments in arrangements which threaten the security of the United States.*

In view of the announced purpose of international communism it may be assumed that, today, any "arrangement" between a Western Hemisphere nation and the Communists threatens the security of the United States.

The fact should never be lost to view that in applying this Doctrine . . . . our government has over and over again driven it as a shield between Europe and the Americas to protect Latin America from the *political* and territorial thrusts of Europe; and this was done at times when . . . the poltical morality of Europe sanctioned, indeed encouraged, the acquisition of territory by force.

For "Europe" in the above read "international communism" to appreciate the importance of maintaining the Doctrine today.

The United States has only been able to give this protection against designing European powers because of its own willingness and determination, if and whenever necessary, to expend its treasure and to sacrifice life to maintain the principles of the doctrine.

Again, read "Communist" for "European" and Mr. Clark's statement undoubtedly applies to the attitude of the American people today.

For, in the final analysis, Monroe's message has always been the expression of the will of the people of the United States— at least since it received the name Doctrine. After the diplomats, the statesmen, the jurists, the international lawyers, the professors and the editors finish pontificating about the meaning of the Doctrine; when the wrangling about whether it is alive or dead dies out—it is the people who decide whether the principle of the Doctrine is valid.

So far, the people have always endorsed the Doctrine when it was properly applied. In 1867 it was popular support for the Doctrine that was the biggest factor in forcing France out of Mexico, although Seward did not quote the Doctrine by name. In 1895 it was the will of the people that demanded its application against England in the Venezuela dispute. In the early 1900s German ambition in the Western Hemisphere was curbed by the knowledge of how the American people felt about their precious Doctrine. And in 1962 the long-dormant Doctrine was revived in the minds of the people to support action against Russia in Cuba.

President Kennedy's action received the unqualified support and well-nigh unanimous acclamation of the people. The nearest thing to a criticism that was heard, even from the opposing political party, was to the effect that action should have been taken sooner. When it comes to the application of the Doctrine against a real threat of foreign aggression, the government has frequently been in the position of the French politician who said, during the French Revolution, "I must hasten to catch up to the people—after all, I am their leader."

So long as there exists in the world an ideology or a political system that opposes the principles of freedom, liberty and independence, to which America is dedicated, there will need to be—and there will be—a Monroe Doctrine to keep such ideas and systems out of the Western Hemisphere. Perhaps future generations will forego the name, but unless America forsakes its sacred ideals, the principles expressed by the Monroe Doctrine cannot be forgotten.

BIBLIOGRAPHY

Alvarez, Alejandro, *The Monroe Doctrine*. New York, Oxford University Press, 1924.
——, *The Monroe Doctrine at the Fourth Pan-American Conference*. Philadelphia, American Academy of Political and Social Sciences, 1911.
Beals, Carleton, *America South*. Philadelphia, J. B. Lippincott Co., 1937.
Bingham, Hiram, "The Monroe Doctrine—An Obsolete Shibboleth." *The Atlantic Monthly*, June, 1913.
Blakeslee, George H., *Latin America*. New York, G. E. Stechert & Co., 1914.
Burr, Robert N., and Hussey, Roland D., *Documents on Inter-American Cooperation*. Philadelphia, University of Pennsylvania Press, 1955.
Cawkell, M. B. R., *The Falkland Islands*. London, Macmillan & Co., Ltd., 1960.
Chapman, Charles C., *A History of the Cuban Republic*. New York, The Macmillan Co., 1927.
Clark, Reuben, *Memorandum on the Monroe Doctrine*. Washington, D. C., U. S. Government Printing Office, 1929.
Cresson, W. P., *Diplomatic Portraits*. Boston, Houghton Mifflin Co., 1923.
——, *The Holy Alliance*. New York Carnegie Endowment of International Peace, Oxford University Press, 1922.
Davis, Richard Harding, *Real Soldiers of Fortune*. New York, Charles Scribner's Sons, 1906.
Duggan, Laurence, *The Americas*. New York, Henry Holt and Co., 1949.
Duggan, Stephen, *The Two Americas—An Interpretation*. New York, Charles Scribner's Sons, 1934.

DuVal, Miles P., *Cadiz to Cathay*. Stanford University, Stanford University Press, 1940.

Foner, Philip S., *A History of Cuba*. New York, International Publishers, 1961.

Hill, Howard C., *Roosevelt and the Caribbean*. Chicago, University of Chicago Press, 1927.

Kirk, Grayson, *The Monroe Doctrine Today*. New York, Farrar and Rinehart, 1941.

MacCorkle, W. A., *The Personal Genesis of the Monroe Doctrine*. New York, G. P. Putnam's Sons, 1923.

Nerval, Gaston, *Autopsy of the Monroe Doctrine*. New York, The Macmillan Co., 1934.

Perkins, Dexter, *A History of the Monroe Doctrine*. Boston, Little, Brown and Co., 1955.

——, *The Monroe Doctrine*. Boston, Harvard University Press, 1927. 3 volumes.

Rippy, Fred, *The Caribbean Danger Zone*. New York, G. P. Putnam's Sons, 1940.

——, *Latin America*. Ann Arbor, The University of Michigan Press, 1958.

——, *Mexico*. Chicago, University of Chicago Press, 1928.

——, *The United States and Mexico*. New York, Alfred A. Knopf, 1924.

Showman, Richard, and Judson, Lyman, *The Monroe Doctrine and the Growth of Western Hemisphere Solidarity*. New York, The H. W. Wilson Co., 1941.

Stark, Harry, *Social and Economics Frontier in Latin America*. Dubuque, Iowa, William E. Brown Co., 1961.

Strobe, Hudson, *The Pageant of Cuba*. New York, Harrison Smith and Robert Haas, 1934.

Thomas, David Y., *One Hundred Years of the Monroe Doctrine*. New York, The Macmillan Co., 1927.

Ugarte, Manuel, *The Destiny of a Continent*. New York, Alfred A. Knopf, 1925.

Wertenbaker, Charles, *A New Doctrine for the Americas*. New York, The Viking Press, 1941.

Whitaker, Arthur Preston, *The U. S. and the Independence of Latin America*. Baltimore, The Johns Hopkins Press, 1941.

Wilson, George Grafton, *The Monroe Doctrine After the War*. Boston, World Peace Foundation, 1918.

American Foreign Policy. Carnegie Endowment for International Peace. Division of Intercourse and Education. Publication No. 17. Washington, D. C.

Economic Defense of the Western Hemisphere, The. A Symposium. American Council of Public Affairs, Washington, D. C., 1941.

Hamilton Facsimiles of Manuscripts, Part I. The Public Opinion
Company, New York, 1896.

International Relations of the United States. The Annals, American
Academy of Political and Social Science, Philadelphia. July,
1914–June, 1924.

Bulletin of the Pan-American Union, Volume 79. Pan-American Union, Washington, D. C., 1945.

Papers of the American Historical Association, Vol. 1. New York,
G. P. Putnam's Sons, 1886.

Treaties and Other International Acts. U. S. Department of State,
U. S. Government Printing Office, Washington, D. C.

Index

DATE DUE

NOV 9 '66	APR 12 '72		
NOV 16 '66	APR 25 '73		
NOV 22 66	NO 21 '77		
NOV 15 '67			
NOV 18 '68			
DEC 2 '68			
NOV 26 '69			
DEC 1 69			
OCT 27 70			
NOV 16 70			
NOV 18 '7			
DEC 2 '70			
JAN 13 '71			
JAN 12 '71			
FEB 1 71			
APR 6 '71			
MAY 3 '71			
DEC 7 '71			
GAYLORD			PRINTED IN U.S.A.